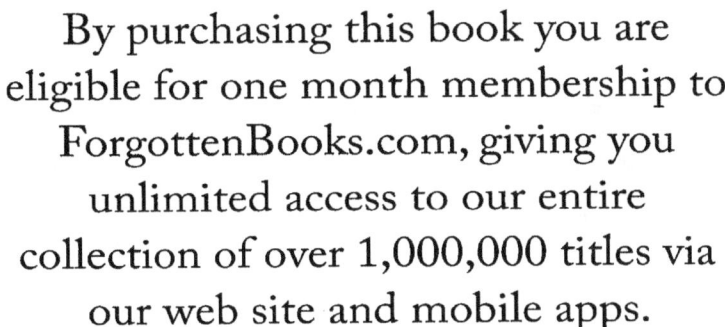

ISBN 978-0-484-37329-6
PIBN 10304173

OFFICE OF THE DIRECTOR

1984 Annual Report
October 1, 1983-September 30, 1984

U.S. DEPARTMENT
OF HEALTH
AND HUMAN SERVICES

National
Institutes of
Health

National
Cancer
Institute

National Cancer Institute

OFFICE OF THE DIRECTOR

1984 Annual Report
October 1, 1983-September 30, 1984

U.S. DEPARTMENT
OF HEALTH
AND HUMAN SERVICES

National
Institutes of
Health

National
Cancer
Institute

Bethesda,
Maryland 20205

National Cancer Institute

NATIONAL CANCER INSTITUTE

Annual Report

October 1, 1983 through September 30, 1984

TABLE OF CONTENTS

Page

Office of Administrative Management

Office of Cancer Communications

Office of the Director for Program Planning and Analysis

OFFICE OF THE ASSOCIATE DIRECTOR
OFFICE OF THE DIRECTOR
NATIONAL CANCER INSTITUTE

PROGRAM ACTIVITIES REPORT

OCTOBER 1, 1983 through September 30, 1984

General Framework of Responsibility

The functions of the Office of the Associate Director can best be described as those which involve scientific coordination among scientific divisions of the National Cancer Institute. The formation and rearrangement of scientific units, the incorporation of new developments in science into intramural management structures, and the general consideration of contract support for intramural research are of major concern. The Frederick Cancer Research Facility system of research and support contracts is a major responsibility. Coordination of intramural science also extends to the questions of outside activities and the determination of patent status rights in derivative inventions.

Intramural Scientific Coordination

Several major areas of activity took place in the past year. These blended basic science expertise in various segments of cancer research to effect major intramural scientific decisions. In general, two major types of events are influenced and modified by the Associate Director. The first is the formation or restructuring of basic science laboratories. This has occurred and is occurring with all Divisions. Close advisory and consulting activity with the Director and Division Directors is mandatory. Eventually a concensus option is reached relative to the final proposed laboratory structure. This is discussed and decided upon by the Executive Committee.

The second element involves inter-laboratory, inter-divisional cooperation on timely topics, usually in breakthrough areas of science. At times, these interactions are intense but not structured. Areas of key national importance may be considered. Close input occurs on a regular basis by pertinent intramural personnel as well as by members of the NCI advisory bodies. The information is transmitted to the Director, NCI, on an ongoing basis, because he makes the final decisions in the areas of dramatic scientific paradigm changes. The commitment of the Institute to new activities results from this input.

A major activity of the past year has been the potential acquisition of the first supercomputer to be dedicated to biomedicine. A reformulation of the Laboratory of Molecular Biology in DCBD was to take place around advanced computing capabilities. In a series of input meetings it became apparent that there is a present and ever-increasing need for supercomputing in several areas of cancer research. The office of the Associate Director collaborated closely with DCBD in selecting a new Laboratory Chief and the acquisition of the instrumentation as well as its support. The location at the FCRF, and the structuring of the operation within NCI's large technical and support contract, was considered to be the most expeditious and advantageous solution.

NCI AIDS Task Force

The original mission was to integrate intramural and extramural research in this area into a cohesive interactive group. The scientific and clinical components blended well. Extramural scientists were brought in on an ad hoc basis to participate in ongoing discussions and planning of future experiments. Because of NCI's past expertise in the area, and because a number of precedents existed in animal models, the area of retrovirus research remained the major target. A great majority of national and international scientists in this area participated in this research thrust. The breakthrough occurred by the finding in Dr. Gallo's laboratory of the probable causative agent of AIDS, a virus named HTLV III, which belongs to the family of human leukemia and lymphoma inducing retroviruses. The large amounts of epidemiological and virological data became convincing to the degree that major HHS moves were initiated to translate these research findings so that practical benefits result as soon as possible.

Several major management decisions resulted from these research findings. The ability to grow the HTLV III virus to large scale predicated efforts in developing an antibody test in multi-million sample quantities to determine past virus exposure so that the national blood supply can be protected. Secondly, virus and its antigens could theoretically serve as a source for a vaccine preparation. To expedite the process, NCI called upon the Technical Support contract at FCRF to immediately scale up HTLV III production so that large (100 liter) amounts of virus could be transferred to licensees in the commercial sector who would actually perform the testing. Successful exponential expansion occurred in the Biological Products Laboratory at FCRF and large scale transfer of reagents occurred. The key element was that no down time resulted from the cession of licenses and the ability of the licensees to start large scale production and testing on their own. Several meetings of NCI personnel took place with the licensees to effect the state-of-the-art information transfer on the antibody tests. A further integrated NCI contribution was that the initial IND development involved NCI personnel working in conjunction with FDA.

The other major management structuring had to do with the organization of the NCI AIDS Task Force itself. Whereas prior to the discovery of the causative agent the interactive discussions dealt with investigative science, subsequent discussion could have an impact on funding decisions. In accordance with normal procedure, the involvement of experts on several divisional BSC's was sought and formal subcommittees of the DCT BSC were established for input on both vaccine development for the eventual prevention of AIDS and for possible interventive measures for those already afflicted. Several meetings with reports to both boards of DCT and DCE have resulted.

Office of the Director Seminars

A formal and defined mechanism for rapid updatiang in the avant garde areas of science is defined by the Office of the Director Continuing Seminar Series. When possible, these are scheduled on a bi-weekly basis. Although the primary purpose is the transmission of novel information in science, other purposes are served as well. For example, controversial claims and observations are evaluated, new intramural findings are discussed in detail, and other timely topics of general interest to NCI which may affect long range planning are considered as well. In FY84, a total of 12 took place.

Outside Activities

The major responsibility is the adjudication of whether an activity by an intramural scientist for a profit or a nonprofit organization represents a potential conflict of interest. The activity is subject to prior signatory approval by the Office of the Associate Director. The decision is next forwarded to the Deputy Director for Intramural Research, NIH, for confirmation.

Up to now, 650 requests were decided upon, or approximately 65 per month, with a projected yearly total of 780. These consisted primarily of scientific lectures and secondarily, of medical practice consults. Specific sets of rules and standard phraseology were developed so that the activity would not be misinterpreted to fall within the realm of consulting which is as yet unacceptable. The rules developed in the previous year were applied regularly. Although NIH considered the possibility of limited nonexclusive consulting with industry, the present status of no formal consulting arrangement was maintained. A number of points such as secrecy, exclusivity, etc. would be difficult to put into practice at NIH. However, the inability to further an intramural scientist's income may have a long range negative impact on NIH in terms of losses to industry and a less competitive recruitment position.

Essentially all approvals from this office were cleared by the subsequent NIH authorizing officials. The discordancy rate was on the order of about 1%. Some of these were precedent setting, because there were no prior guidelines. After discussion with Building 1 or legal counsel, and further arbitration, Building 1 prevailed at times, but the converse also occurred.

Patents

Another related function of the Office of the Associate Director is to be involved in the generation of inventions by intramural scientists. This ranges from encouraging or initiating the patent process to determining the status of potential or actual inventions which were wholly, or in part, developed under Federal research support. The decision process falls into two categories; the first of which is an evaluation of the invention status. This is usually generated as a request via OMAR. These requests are either considered directly or funneled to individual NCI experts for assessment. The second assessment involves the ruling evaluating whether the petitioner who is generally seeking exclusivity or greater rights should be so granted. The laws have changed on this subject within the past year and a new set of rules have been developed.

Two NCI inventions applied for this year had a major impact on the functioning of the entire PHS. These have to do with the development of production of the AIDS causative agent, HTLV III, and the antibody detection tests. The OAD was directly involved as the stimulus for patenting these inventions and monitored the entire process until the release of the information to the public to protect the foreign patent rights. Further possible inventions which are expected to result in this critical area are closely scrutinized by this office.

NCI Monoclonal Antibody Working Group

The mission of the working group is to integrate and facilitate the continuum of activities which begin at the bench and terminate in the treatment of the patient. The group which is headed by the Associate Director represents a cross-divisional scientific activity of NCI. A combined input on this multidisciplinary activity continues to be manifest. The skills of participants include topics such as: theoretical immunology, basic hybridoma technology, cytokine activity, anti-idiotypes, tumor cell-surface antigens, "arming" technology involving both radiometal chelates and toxins, growth factors and potential oncogene products, and clinical expertise in the diagnosis and treatment of tumors with monoclonal antibodies.

Frederick Cancer Research Facility

The Associate Director has overall responsibility for the operation of the Frederick Cancer Research Facility (FCRF), a Government-owned/Contractor-operated facility located in Frederick, Maryland. On-site NCI management is through a General Manager who reports directly to the Associate Director. In addition, the Research Contracts Branch maintains a section level unit at the FCRF headed by a Contracting Officer who works with the General Manager to assure effective management of the facility.

The FCRF houses both intramural and contractor research programs. The intramural programs represent laboratories associated with each of the three research divisions in the NCI, as well as laboratories of the NINCDS and NIAID. During the current reporting period, the Laboratory of Molecular Oncology, a major program in the DCE, was relocated to the FCRF and commenced operations in a newly renovated facility. Several small intramural units also were relocated during the year. At the present time, approximately 350 Government employees are located at the FCRF.

All NCI research programs at the FCRF undergo peer review. Intramural laboratories are reviewed by divisional Boards of Scientific Counselors on the same basis as laboratories located at the Bethesda campus. Contractor research programs are reviewed by the FCRF Advisory Committee. This Committee was chartered by the Director, NCI, and is composed of senior non-Government scientists, including representatives of Division Boards of Scientific Counselors.

During the current reporting period, a new Principal Investigator for the Basic Research Program was brought on board following a lengthy selection process. He immediately began recruiting new personnel to augment the scientific staff in accordance with recommendations of the FCRF Advisory Committee. Under the leadership of the new Principal Investigator and with the Committee's concurrence, the emphasis of the Basic Research Program is being channeled toward areas of research identified as critical to the needs and mission of the NCI. Specific emphasis will be placed on molecular aspects of carcinogenesis, including the identification and characterization of oncogene sequences in human tumor DNA's and the isolation and characterization of oncogene products. Molecular techniques relating to oncogene induction and expression will be applied in laboratories studying the mechanism of chemical carcinogenesis. On-going programs will be expanded in areas relating to the role of cellular growth factors in carcinogenesis and the relationship between these factors and oncogenes. Programs to develop new cloning and expression vectors will be augmented by the addition of a laboratory of yeast genetics.

A major accomplishment during the current reporting period was the implementation of a shared service support program in the Operations and Technical Support contract. This program furnishes technical support in areas such as chemical synthesis and analysis, electron microscopy, biological products, mycoplasma testing, nucleic acid and protein synthesis, fluorescent cell sorting, clinical immunology, photography, graphics, microbial mutagenesis, histology/pathology, and monoclonal antibody production and purification. Technical services also are made available to intramural investigators located at the Bethesda campus. The shared service program operates on a pay-back system whereby the user laboratories are charged direct costs for services. The program is monitored by the General Manager who receives reports from users on a monthly basis. The success of the program was evidenced by the progressive increase in demand for services and the verified high quality of the work produced. New shared service areas to be implemented include plasmic production and nucleic acid and protein sequencing.

The FCRF serves the important function of providing a means for the NCI to deploy, with minimal delay, technical expertise in critical areas as they are identified by the Institute. The soundness of this approach was demonstrated vividly during the current reporting period when the resources of the FCRF were brought to bear on the problem of HTV and its role in human AIDS. The Operations and Technical Support contractor, through the shared service program, furnished extensive technical support to intramural investigators in delineating the putative etiologic role of HTLV III in AIDS. The Contractor was also given the responsibility of producing HTLV III infected cell cultures for distribution to companies licensed by the Government to develop diagnostic tests.

In the administrative area, new procedures and reports were developed by the Operations and Technical Support and the Computer Service contractors to provide intramural programs with improved monitoring systems for their expenditures at the FCRF. Studies were undertaken to upgrade building maintenance procedures at the facility and to improve the energy utilization efficiency of individual buildings. In addition, plans are being implemented to renovate laboratory areas for new Basic Research Programs as well as to provide additional P3 containment facilities for work with HTLV and related infectious agents. The FCRF has taken the lead in requiring that work with putative human etiologic agents be carried out in approved containment laboratories.

<u>Research Aspects of the OD Unit at FCRF</u>

The Research Unit within the Office of the Director represents continuation of past scientific commitments in the general area of carcinogenesis. Many of these studies are derived from the initial observations that viral murine leukemias were probably caused by polytropic recombinant murine leukemia viruses (Rm-MuLV) rather than the input standard MuLV (e-MuLV). Rm-MuLV were identified in mice inoculated with e-MuLV and were regularly isolated from both the preleukemic and leukemic state. The newly-generated Rm-MuLV's derived from known e-MuLV were examined by peptide map analysis of the envelope gene product and restriction endonuclease mapping of virus genomes. It was shown that a given e-MuLV will specifically recombine with only a few of many available endogenous provirus sequences present in the mouse chromosome. Further, Rm-MuLV that have large substitutions in the envelope gene have different peptide maps than those with smaller substitutions. These observations suggest that the generation of Rm-MuLV is not a random event.

A second area of investigation in the laboratory unit involves the molecular characterization of viral envelope gene products produced by a number of retroviruses. In the area of radiation-induced leukemias, it was found that cells derived from these leukemias produce viral envelope gene products but not other viral structural or enzymatic polypeptides. Analyses of the mRNA from these leukemia cells showed that the genetic sequences being expressed were purely endogenous defected provirus sequences. Peptide map studies showed these gp70s were unique and only partially resembled known Rm-MuLV that have been proposed as causative agents in murine leukemogenesis. Thus, physical agents such as ionizing radiation have been shown to activate the expression of endogenous retroviral sequences in the absence of the replication of competent e-MuLV or Rm-MuLV. The skills obtained from the analysis of small permutations in the envelope have been applied to the studies of rapidly mutating retroviruses such as the equine infectious leukemia virus.

A third area of interest revolves about the observation that mouse factor in the very low density lipoprotein fraction that inactivátes only certain types of MuLV very efficiently. This factor has been proposed as a mechanism by which the mouse naturally resists the proliferation of potentially oncogenic retroviruses. The interaction between factor and virus is mediated through a polypeptide component present on the surface of virions. The specific domains of the factor molecules involved in the interaction will be determined by competition assays using protease fragments from interacting polypeptides. Early data indicate that the action spectrum of this entity may be extended to inactivate other retroviruses.

Efforts have been established to characterize the replication of HTLV III in human thymocytes. Simple quantal assays for the virus are being developed. The viral envelope gene products may be released into cell culture fluids in the form of nonparticular polypeptides. This project will examine cell culture fluids for the presence of viral-specific polypeptides that interact with sera obtained from human patients infected with HTLV III to determine whether these constitute materials feasible for vaccines. Monoclonal antibodies are being developed to the envelopes of members of the HTLV family for typing and diagnostic purposes.

Studies to delineate the antigens of herpes simplex virus (HSV) types 1 and 2 were extended using a battery of monoclonal antibodies produced against the two viruses. These studies were carried out in collaboration with PRI scientists at the NCI-FCRF. A major finding was that the 130,000 mw glycoprotein gC, which was reported to be type specific for HSV-1 by several groups, actually contains epitopes which cross-react with an HSV-2 glycoprotein (gF) of 75,000 mw. The relationship between gC and gF was shown using a monoclonal antibody (104-S) made against HSV-2. Analysis by RIP-PAGE indicated that the 104-S antibody immunoprecipitated the 75,000 mw glycoprotein gF from HSV-2 infected cells and the 130,000 mw glycoprotein gC from HSV-1 infected cells. The peptide maps of the 130,000 mw gC immunoprecipitated and 104-S (anti-HSV-2 gF) were identical. The finding that gC is not type-specific for HSV-1 was confirmed by other laboratories and is significant since it indicates that gC cannot be employed for typing antibodies to HSV-1.

Studies carried out in collaboration with LBI and BRMP scientists demonstrated that activated human monocytes can selectively lyse HSV-2 infected cells. Monocyte activation was accomplished using lysosomes carrying human gamma interferon, lymphokines or a lipophilic derivative of muramyl dipeptide. Additional studies demonstrated that activated, but not unactivated, macrophages can selectively lyse HSV-2 infected cells. These studies have potential significance with respect to treatment modalities for human infections by HSV or other viruses.

Office of Laboratory Animal Science (LAS)

This Office maintains the responsibility for animal research policy and logistical support of intramural animal research programs. This division-coordinated approach at the OD level has aided the effective implementation of uniform animal research practices at NCI in accord with both humane practices and recommendations contained in the ILAR, NAS, Guide for the Care and Use of Laboratory Animals. The Central Animal Resources unit within the Office of Laboratory Animal Science performs direct basic care and support services, quarantine, and health surveillance of research animals for NCI.

To resolve the myriad of inconsistencies in remote animal holding areas, LAS is coordinating the NCI trend to operating small centralized facilities within buildings or areas within buildings. The 5,000 square foot DCT Central Animal Facility in Building 37 initiated in 1980 became a reality this year and represents the most recent effort to consolidate and upgrade animal holding space. The Building 10/ACRF DCT Central Animal Facility on the 13th floor is managed by LAS inclusive of providing all attendent laboratory animal services. The ACRF is also fully operational as a centralized facility. A program of centralized management for decentralized animal holding areas is underway within the divisions.

LAS is an intramural focal point for animal and animal cell monitoring for common animal contaminants to meet the objective of MI-3043-1 on the "Introduction of Rodents and Rodent Products." In this respect, LAS established a mechanism available to all NCI investigators introducing such animal and products both from the United States research communities and commercial sources as well as overseas. In addition to providing laboratory analysis, facilities for isolation, quarantine and defining animals is managed by LAS at a lease site off campus.

LAS is active in the resolution of animal research grant discrepancies not in compliance with the Office of Protection from Research Risks by reviewing site visit reports with Executive Secretaries and Project Officers and offering mutually agreeable solutions to inadequacies rather than forwarding problems to OPRR. LAS also consults and collaborates with the Research Facilities Branch on compliance and construction of NCI animal facility items dealing with possible action for uniform standards.

An Animal Handler Surveillance Program with the Occupational Medical Services whereby animal technicians will be assured of automatic review and call-up on their health status when involved with research animals is monitored by LAS.

LAS continued to participate in various NIH level animal committees; i.e., NIH Genetic Advisory Committee, NIH-FCRF Animal Advisory Committee, NIH Trans Coordinating Committee for Research Animal Resources, and the NIH Animal Research Committee. Many of NCI animal standard operating policies and research protocol review mechanisms are being incorporated into NIH practice. The NCI MI-3040 on "Care and Use of Animals in NCI Intramural Research" was used as the model for the recently approved NIH MI-3040-2 "Animal Care and Use in the Intramural Program."

Personnel within LAS continue to participate in seminars and programs of associations dealing with laboratory animal science; i.e., AALAS, ACLAM, AVMA, ILAR, to facilitate information exchange and training.

LAS continues to serve as the focal point for the evaluation and design of proposed renovations and/or construction of animal research facilities. In addition to consultation and technical assistance, LAS is a resource to management and staff for laboratory animal requirements and intramural logistical support.

References

Fischinger, P.J.: Current developments and future prevention of the acquired immune deficiency syndrome (AIDS). In: (Ed. Hickey, R.C., and Clark, R.L.) Current Problems in Cancer. Year Book Medical Publishers, Chicago, In press, 1984.

Fischinger, P.J.: Molecular Mechanisms of Leukaemogenesis by Murine Leukemia Viruses. In: (Eds. Goldman, J.M., and Jarrett, J.O.) Mechanisms of Viral Leukaemogenesis, Chapter 5. Churchill Livinstone, London, 1984, pp 89-134.

Fischinger, P.J.: Perspectives and prospects of molecular biology in the control of human malignancies. Proceedings of the International Research Conference on RNA Tumor Viruses in Human Cancer. Denver, Colorado, June, 1984. In Press, 1984.

Fischinger, P.J.: Primary prevention of acquired immune deficiency syndrome (AIDS) and other human T cell leukemia (HTLV) associated diseases. In: (Eds. DeVita, V.T. Jr., Hellman, S., and Rosenberg, S.A.) CANCER, Principles and Practice of Oncology, 2nd Edition. J. B. Lippincott, Philadelphia, Pennsylvania. In press, 1984.

Fischinger, P.J. and DeVita, V.T. Jr.: Governance of Science at the National Cancer Institute: Perceptions and Opportunities in Oncogene Research. Cancer Res., In press, 1984.

Fischinger, P.J., Dunlop, N.M., Dekaban, G.A., and Robey, W.G.: The Role of Viral and Cellular Recombinational Events in Murine Leukemia. In: (Ed. Murphy, G.P.) Transplantation Proceedings. Grune and Stratton, Orlando, Florida, 1984, pp. 428-434.

Fischinger, P.J., Dunlop, N.M., and Robey, W.G.: Generation of recombinant murine leukemia virus de novo: Alternative models of leukemogenesis. In: (Eds. Neth, R., Gallo, R., Greaves, M., Moore, and Winkler, E.) Haematology and Blood Transfusion, Vol. 28. Modern Trends in Human Leukemia V. Springer-Verlag, Berlin, Heidelberg, 1983, pp. 261-269.

Fischinger, P.J., Dunlop, N.M., and Robey, W.G.: Pathogenesis and virus content of lymphomas induced by pure ecotropic Graffi murine leukemia virus. The Henry S. Kaplan Memorial Issue. Int. J. Radiat., Oncol., Biol. and Phys. In press, 1984.

Fischinger, P.J., Dunlop, N.M., Robey, W.G., and Schafer, W.G.: Generation of thymotropic envelope gene recombinant virus and induction of lymphoma by ecotropic Moloney murine leukemia virus. Virology, In press, 1984.

Koff, W.C., Fidler, I.J., Showalter, S.D., Chakrabarty, M.K., Hampar, B., Ceccorulli, L.M., and Kleinerman, E.S.: Human monocytes activated by immunomodulators in liposomes lyse herpesvirus-infected but not normal cells. Science 224: 1007-1009, 1984.

Koff, W.C., Showalter, S.D., Seniff, D.A., and Hampar, B.: Lysis of herpesvirus-infected cells by macrophages activated with free or liposome-encapsulated lymphokine produced by a murine T cell hybridoma. Inf. Immun. 42: 1067-1072, 1983.

Robey, W.G., Dekaban, G.A., Ball, J.A., and Fischinger, M.D.: Envelope glycoproteins of polytropic recombinant viruses derived from Moloney murine leukemia viruses display common features. Virology, In press, 1984.

Zweig, M., Heilman, C.J.,Jr., Bladen, S.V., Showalter, S.D., and Hampar, B.: Detection in antisera of antibodies that cross-react with herpes simplex virus type 1 glycoprotein gC. Inf. Immun. 41: 482-487, 1983.

Zweig, M., Showalter, S.D., Bladen, S.V., Heilman, C. J., Jr., and Hampar, B.: Herpes simplex virus type 2 glycoprotein gF and type 1 glycoprotein gC have related antigenic determinants. J. Virol. 47: 185-192, 1983.

OFFICE OF THE ASSISTANT DIRECTOR

OFFICE OF THE DIRECTOR

PROGRAM ACTIVITIES REPORT

October 1, 1983, through September 30, 1984

One major responsibility of the Office of the Assistant Director (AD) is to administer and support the functions of the President's Cancer Panel. The Panel has served as a forum for both the scientific community and the public, and has affecte the initiation of new programs and the implementation of existing priorities. The AD serves as the Executive Secretary to the Panel.

The President's Cancer Panel consists of Dr. Armand Hammer, Chairman, who has been reappointed by the White House for a second term in that office, and two other members, Dr. William P. Longmire, Jr., and Dr. John A. Montgomery.

During this 12-month period, the Panel held five meetings. One meeting was in Bethesda and four were regional meetings in New York City, Birmingham, Los Angeles, and San Francisco.

In 1982, the President's Cancer Panel initiated a study of the Peer Review System, and the NIH grant mechanisms available to established research investigators. Following hearings and consultations with members of the scientific community at meetings conducted around the country, these studies were completed this year. The Report of the President's Cancer Panel on Peer Review by the NIH was transmitted by Dr. DeVita on March 5, 1984, to the Director of the NIH. The report contains a series of proposals intended to strengthen the Peer Review System, and requests they be considered for implementation.

The initiative undertaken by the Panel Task Force to establish a new grant mechanism for the support of outstanding investigators with proven productive careers, culminated in the announcement by the Division of Research Grants on March 30, 1984 of the new R-35 grant, the National Cancer Institute (NCI) Outstanding Investigator Grant. One hundred and twenty-five applications from the scientific community have been received in this first year of the award mechanism.

A new initiative undertaken by the President's Cancer Panel this year is an examination of mechanisms utilized by cancer centers to reduce cancer mortality in their communities. The Panel has embarked on a series of hearings throughout the country to examine the strengths of the cancer centers, and to help identify areas that nee further attention.

The AD is also responsible for the Office of Medical Applications of Cancer Researc (OMACR), and maintains liaison with the NIH Office of Medical Applications of Research (OMAR). As NCI representative to OMAR, the AD is a member of the Coordinating Committee on Assessment and Transfer of Technology (CCATT) for NIH. During FY 1984, OMACR processed numerous evaluations of patent applications from grantees, contractors, and intramural scientists. OMAR also supports the consensus development programs and other technology transfer activities at the NIH. A major activit during this period was the NCI-sponsored Consensus Development Conference on Precur sors to Malignant Melanoma which was held at the Lister Hill Center of the NIH,

October 24-26, 1983. The objective of the conference was to evaluate the issues concerning the current technology and arrive at a consensus statement useful to health care providers and the public at large.

This conference highlighted an important advance in our understanding of melanoma through the identification of a familial syndrome in which multiple dysplastic nevi are associated with development of melanomas. The investigation of patients with this syndrome affords an opportunity not only to advance our knowledge of the biology of melanoma but also to aid the identification of treatable precursor lesions and early melanomas. The result may be a reduction in mortality in these patients.

Planning has begun for an NCI Consensus Development Conference on Limb-Sparing Treatment of Adult Soft Tissue and Osteogenic Sarcomas, which is scheduled for December 3-5, 1984. This planning has been coordinated by Dr. Alfred E. Chang in close collaboration with others on the staff of the Division of Cancer Treatment.

Activities of the Office of the AD this year have included continued responsibilities related to three radiation research committees. The Assistant Director served as Executive Secretary for the Interagency Radiation Research Committee, chaired by Dr. James B. Wyngaarden, NIH Director, which held its final meeting in January 1984. A member of the staff of the Office of the AD, Dr. Victor Zeve, is Executive Secretary and provides additional support for two committees established pursuant to the Orphan Drug Act (PL97-414), passed in January 1983. Dr. Zeve is Executive Secretary for the Ad Hoc Working Group to Develop Radioepidemiological Tables as per Section 7(b) of PL97-414, and also for the committee to report on the analysis of thyroid cancer in relation to iodine-131 exposure, as required by section 7(a) of the above law. These activities are coordinated with the Office of the Director, NIH, and the Office of the Secretary, DHHS.

Additional functions of the Office of the AD include signatory responsibilities for NCI contract negotiations; the review of Confidential Statements of Employment and Financial Interests; and, as Deputy Ethics Counselor for NCI, the AD also affirms the absence of conflicts of interest for the staff of the Institute, following a review of activities and holdings reported by the employees.

OFFICE OF INTERNATIONAL AFFAIRS (OIA)

OFFICE OF THE DIRECTOR

NATIONAL CANCER INSTITUTE

Report of International Activities

October 1, 1983 - September 30, 1984

I. INTRODUCTION

The National Cancer Institute continues to contribute significantly to the improvement of the basic quality of life because of its long tradition of involvement in the international arena for cancer research. The interest of the National Cancer Institute in the cancer problems of other nations has contributed to the establishment of a concerted international effort in the war on cancer. The National Cancer Act has intensified the commitment of the NCI to the international team approach toward the control, prevention, and ultimate eradication of cancer as a major crippler and killer disease of a large segment of the world's population.

By virtue of the prevalent international effort against cancer, striking variations in the incidence, and mortality of a wide range of specific organ cancers are now well recognized and, in some instances, the geographic, environmental, and socioeconomic causes have been established for excess rates of cancer incidence in certain regions of the world. The derivation of cause-effect relationships stems from studies in those countries of the world where the population is at low risk for a given type of cancer, thereby establishing a "baseline" rate for that particular cancer type. Subsequently, a high rate of incidence for that same cancer in other countries can be assumed to be associated with the factors endemic in the environment of those countries.

Through its participation in activities of the international cancer science community, the National Cancer Institute benefits ultimately from the rapid advances in basic research throughout the world and their translation into application for the clinical management, control, and prevention of cancer. The ultimate gain from such collaborative cancer research efforts between the NCI and its international counterparts is a tangible improvement in the quality and quantity of health services to millions of people over the world.

The contribution of NCI to the international struggle against cancer includes: (1) the support of cancer research in foreign countries by scientists who are highly qualified by virtue of a unique expertise; (2) the support of cooperative research programs, principally through bilateral agreements with foreign government institutions or organizations; (3) maintenance of liaison and research collaboration with international organizations and agencies that have well-defined objectives in cancer research and cancer prevention; (4) the support of training of foreign scientists in the United States as well as of the interaction of American scientists with colleagues in foreign laboratories; and (5) the management and operation of an International Cancer Information Center for promoting and facilitating, on a worldwide basis, the exchange of information for cancer research, treatment, care and management of patients, and cancer control and/or prevention.

II. BILATERAL AGREEMENTS AND OTHER COUNTRY-TO-COUNTRY ACTIVITIES

Cooperative cancer research programs under formal government-to-government treaties and other forms of bilateral agreement comprise a major segment of the international activities of the NCI. The first of these cooperative cancer research agreements was established on May 23, 1972, with the signing of the USA-USSR Agreement for Cooperation in the Fields of Medical Science and Public Health. Subsequently, additional bilateral programs were formalized between the NCI and the Japanese Society for the Promotion of Science (1974); the Institute of Oncology, Warsaw, Poland (1974), under the USA-Polish People's Republic

Agreement; in 1975 with the French Institut National de la Sante et de la Recherche Medicale (INSERM) under the earlier NIH Agreement with INSERM; the Cairo Cancer Institute (1976) under the aegis of the Agreement between the USA and the Arab Republic of Egypt; the Ministry of Science and Technology of the Federal Republic of Germany (1976); the Cancer Institute (Hospital), Chinese Academy of Medical Sciences, under the USA-People's Republic of China Accord for Cooperation in Science and Technology (1979); the National Cancer Institute of Milan and the Institute of Oncology of Genoa, Italy (1980); the National Institute of Oncology, Budapest, Hungary (1981); and the Victor Babes Institute, Bucharest, Romania (1983).

The following sections relate to NCI's bilateral activities and the progress that has been achieved through these cooperative efforts.

COOPERATION WITH THE SOVIET UNION

From inception in 1972, until late 1981, the American-Soviet collaborative cancer activities spanned a scientific spectrum which included cancer treatment, tumor immunology, viral oncology, the genetic aspects of neoplasia, epidemiology, cancer pathomorphology, cancer control measures and technologies, and the role of cancer centers in the education and training of personnel in health fields and the lay public. These broad approaches were modified and the objectives were restructured in September 1981. Thus, the scientific areas of cancer treatment, carcinogenesis, and cancer prevention now constitute the priority areas for continuing collaboration between American and Soviet cancer specialists. Annual meetings of delegations have been deemphasized in favor of individual scientific exchanges

Although no Soviet scientists are expected to travel to the United States during this year, NCI has proposed to the Soviet counterparts the visits of three U.S. scientists for individual scientific exchanges to the Soviet Union.

Collection of patient data is not complete on the Soviet side from the joint study between the University of Maryland Cancer Center and the All-Union Oncologic Scientific Center associated with the Phase I clinical and pharmacological evaluation of carboplatin (GBDGA; NSC 241240). However, encouraging results have been obtained in a similar Phase I trial conducted at NCI.

COOPERATION WITH JAPAN

In March 1983, the Prime Minister of Japan announced a proposed plan to initiate a 10-year Comprehensive Cancer Control Program in FY 1984. This new program will, in effect, approximately double the amount of the current support of cancer research by the Japanese government. The Ministry of Health and Welfare; the Ministry of Education, Science and Culture; and the Science and Technology Agency will equally share the new monies for the support of new initiatives at leading Japanese research institutions and centers of excellence. In addition, the three governmental agencies will increase their respective efforts in international cooperation by inviting foreign scientists to engage in collaborative research activities in Japan, as well as sending young Japanese scientists abroad for study and training in basic and clinical cancer research. It is anticipated that the US-Japan Cooperative Cancer Research Program, which is sponsored by the National Cancer Institute and the Japan Society for the Promotion of Science (JSPS), will work in concert with the new Comprehensive

Cancer Control Program.

In October, the NCI and the JSPS signed an agreement to renew the US-Japan Cooperative Cancer Research Program for an additional five years of international cooperation, beginning in April 1984 through March 1989.

Etiology Program Area

A seminar on "Carcinogenicity, Mutagenicity and Metabolism of Heterocyclic Amines" was held at the East West Center in Honolulu, Hawaii, in February 1984. The seminar was organized by Dr. Snorri S. Thorgeirsson, NCI, and Dr. Shigeaki Sato, National Cancer Center Research Institute, Tokyo, Japan. In attendance were 7 Japanese and 7 American scientists to discuss the latest research on heterocyclic amines. Papers were presented on the identification and characterization of genotoxic compounds in cooked beef, heterocyclic amines in cooked foods, other mutagens in food, mutagens in cooked beef, and *in vivo* carcinogenicity of heterocyclic amines. During the session on the Metabolic and Genotoxicity of Heterocyclic Amines, several interesting and informative discussions were held on the analytical methods of heterocyclic amines; the metabolites of heterocyclic amines in bile, feces, and urine; *in vitro* metabolism of heterocyclic amines; the organic chemistry and formation of DNA adducts by heterocyclic amines; model mutagens from cooked beef; the formation of MeI Qx and other related mutagens from heating mixtures of amino acids and glucose; and the heterocyclic amines in Salmonella/hepatocyte system. Very active discussions were also held on the relationship of the basic data on heterocyclic amines to practicality of application for prevention and control of cancer. The proceedings of the meeting are being prepared for publication.

The conference on "Eukaryotic DNA Replication and Repair" was held at Stanford University, California, in March 1984. The meeting was organized by Dr. David Korn, Department of Pathology, Stanford University Medical Center, and Dr. Katsuro Koike, Cancer Institute, Japanese Foundation for Cancer Research, Tokyo. Invited participants included 11 Japanese and 15 American scientists. Topics presented at the conference included the latest work on DNA polymerase-alpha, DNA primase, DNA polymerase-beta and gamma and terminal transferase, model viral DNA replication systems which included adenovirus and SV40, mitochrondrial DNA replication, and the mechanisms of DNA damage and repair.

During the past year, under the Scientist Exchange segment of the Program, a cell biologist from the National Cancer Center Research Institute in Tokyo spent two months at the Department of Biology, Yale University, to engage in joint research on the effect of microinjection of biological materials into mammalian embryonic cells. Materials used included purified poly ADP-ribose, monoclonal antibodies against poly ADP-ribose, and gene or monoclonal antibodies against poly ADP-ribose polymerase to study cell differentiation, transformation, and DNA repair.

A biochemist from the National Cancer Center Research Institute spent two weeks at the Department of Chemistry, University of Hawaii, to collect, purify, and prepare derivatives of aplysiatoxin, a potent tumor promoter found in seaweed found in the waters surrounding the Hawaiian Islands. These compounds are interesting tumor promoters on experimental animals.

A virologist from the Institute of Medical Sciences, Tokyo University, spent one month at the Salk Institute in California to discuss and learn the technique to purify adenoviral gene products and to study the mechanisms of cell transformation.

A biophysicist from the National Cancer Center Research Institute spent three weeks at the Department of Biological Sciences, Stanford University, to learn the techniques to measure thymine glycol, using specific monoclonal antibodies. The technique will be used to study DNA damage and repair in experiments on carcinogenicity of free-radical forming compounds.

A molecular biologist form the Saitama Cancer Center Research Institute spent one month at the Biology Department, University of Utah in Salt Lake City, to learn the new technique of gene transfer by microinjection. In addition, he discussed the nature of carcinogens and tumor promoters in their ability to induce enzymatic systems which enhances genetic recombination and possible association with cell transformation.

A molecular biologist from the Institute of Medical Sciences, Tokyo University, spent 3 months in the Laboratory of Molecular Biology, NCI, to discuss the mechanism of malignant transformation and to collaborate on the isolation of monoclonal antibodies against oncogenic products of avian retroviruses. These antibodies will be used to identify and characterize the target proteins involved in malignant transformation.

A senior investigator from the NCI was invited to participate as a lecturer in a workshop on carcinogenesis sponsored by the International Union Against Cancer (UICC) at the Institute for Medical Sciences, Tokyo University. He visited with several Japanese researchers who are working on biological carcinogenesis and on RNA and DNA tumor viruses. He also visited the National Cancer Center Research Institute to meet with the senior staff members to discuss the research activities of the Institute. The quality of research being done at these two institutions is very impressive, with much of their work at the forefront of carcinogenesis research.

Another NCI investigator participated in the UICC Workshop and presented lectures on cell transformation. He visited several laboratories to discuss recent data on growth factors produced by transformed cells. He also visited the National Cancer Center Research Institute to exchange ideas on oncogene studies and make arrangements to exchange tissue culture cell lines. He visited laboratories at the Cancer Institute and the Institute of Medical Sciences. Later, he visited the Protein Research Institute, Osaka University, to present a seminar on the growth and modulating factors released by the MoSV-transformed murine cells.

Biology and Diagnosis Program Area

The seminar on "Oncogene Products and Neoplastic Cell Growth" was held in October 1983 in Washington, D.C. The meeting was organized by Dr. Benoit de Crombrugghe, Laboratory of Molecular Biology, NCI, and Dr. Yoji Ikawa, Cancer Institute and the Institute for Physical and Chemical Research, Tokyo. There were 7 Japanese and 10 American scientists who presented their work at this seminar. The main topics discussed were the generation of viral and cellular oncogenes, mechanisms of oncogene activation, cellular pathways for transformation, growth factors, cell-surface receptors, and the potential use of receptors for drug targeting.

The seminar on "Immunogenetic Analysis of the Expression of Tumor Antigens and Responses to Tumors" was held in La Jolla, California, in late October 1983. The organizers were Dr. Richard J. Hodes, Immunology Branch, NCI, and Dr. Toshiyuki Hamaoka, Institute for Cancer Research, Osaka University. In attendance were 8 Japanese and 11 American immunologists, who presented their latest research data on tumor immunology. The subjects presented at the seminar included the immunology and molecular biology of tumor antigens, focusing on the identification and characterization of tumor-specific antigens and their relation to the transformation event; the biology of host-tumor immune interaction; T cell differentiation and regulation; characterization of lymphokines; and preclinical approaches to tumor immunology.

A Japanese immunologist from the Institute for Cancer Research, Osaka University, visited the National Cancer Institute and the Dana-Farber Cancer Institute in Boston to discuss and exchange information about immunologic manipulation of tumor immunotherapy with his collaborating colleagues. He also presented a seminar on the latest research on tumor immunology which is being done at Osaka University. He learned the new techniques for the analysis of gene coding for tumor antigens. At the Dana-Farber Cancer Institute he presented a seminar on the functional heterogeneity of tumor antigens capable of inducing distinct host response.

A pathologist from the Sapporo Medical College spent three weeks visiting immunologists at Stanford University, UCLA, and the Memorial Sloan-Kettering Cancer Center in New York to discuss the use of antilymphocyte monoclonal antibodies for immunotherapy of leukemia, production of monoclonal antibodies to tumor related antigens, and the significance of T cell response to human cancers.

A pathologist from Hokkaido University Medical School spent one month at the Frederick Cancer Research Facility, NCI, to learn and discuss the latest technique for the analysis of oncogenes and in situ hybridization for regional gene mapping. Techniques will be used to produce antibodies against tumor cell surface antigens.

A geneticist from the National Institute of Genetics, Shizuoka, Japan, visited the Laboratory of Molecular Genetics, NICHHD, to discuss and learn about the technical problems involved with the DNA manipulation of mouse genomes. He also presented a seminar on the genetic status of Japanese wild mouse and and their H-2 antigens. In addition, he visited other laboratories, including California Institute of Technology and Harvard Medical School to discuss latest studies on sequencing DNA nucleotide bases and the sequencing and mapping of mouse oncogene.

A senior immunologist from the Dana-Farber Cancer Institute, Harvard Medical School, Boston, attended the 15th International Congress of Immunology in Kyoto, Japan, and participated at a workshop on "T-T Cell Interaction During the Induction of Cytotoxic T-cell Response and Long-term Culture of the T-killer Cells." He also participated in the US-Japan Immunology Workshop. In addition, he visited the Institute for Cancer Research, Osaka University, to discuss the latest advances in tumor immunotherapy. He had an excellent opportunity to meet with other leading Japanese immunologists and to learn of their research activities. He also met and interviewed several young scientists interested in studying in the U.S.

Cancer Treatment Program Area

The Annual Program Review Meeting on Cancer Treatment was held in Tokyo in February 1984. The meeting was organized by Dr. Yoshio Sakurai and Dr. Saul Schepartz. At the meeting, 7 American and 18 Japanese participants presented papers; in addition, there were 15 observers from various Japanese institutions.

The first session was devoted to New Approach to Screening, which included presentation on the selection of compounds for screening, preclinical results, stem cell assay, and the rational approach to evaluation of responsiveness of human tumor xenografts to chemotherapy. The session on Fluorinated Pyrimidines discussed the antitumor activity of phthalidyl 5-FU on experimental animal tumors, phase II study of oral 5'-deoxyfluorouridine (UFT) a combination of 5-FU derivative with uracil and UFT, and a new anticancer drug and its clinical application. The session on Differentiation Inducers focused on research on differentiating agents and new approaches to chemotherapy of myeloid leukemia by inducers of terminal differentiation of leukemia cells. Sessions on Biological Response Modifiers were primarily based on the current research on interferon, clinical trials of interferons, and monoclonal antibody research in Japan and in the U.S. Discussions on new drugs included presentations on palmitoyl cytosine arabinoside, a new derivative of mitomycin-C, a new imidazole derivative (SM-108), a new platinum complex, (1-OHP), Mitoxantrone, THP-adriamycin, and other new drugs which are being tested in the U.S. and Japan. The final session was focused on the current results on the incidence and treatment of gastric cancer in Japan and in the U.S.

In May 1984, a seminar on "Advances and New Techniques in Radiation Oncology Research" was held at the University of Washington in Seattle. The organizers were Dr. Mitsuaki Abe, Department of Radiology, Kyoto University, and Dr. Glenn Sheline, Department of Radiation Oncology, University of California, San Francisco. In attendance were 13 Japanese and 17 American radiologists and physicists. The three-day meeting included extensive and intensive discussions on Fast Neutron Beam Radiotherapy, which included the latest clinical data; the use of computers in treatment planning; hyperthermia and radiotherapy, including experimental and clinical data; intraoperative radiotherapy in treating rectal carcinoma and other gastrointestinal malignancies; latest experimental results on the use of radiation sensitizers; dose fractionation effects in normal and tumor tissues; and total body irradiation for bone marrow transplantation in the treatment of leukemia and malignant lymphomas. In addition, the seminar participants were given a tour of the University of Washington Cancer Center and the new Clinical Neutron Beam Therapy Facility.

A medical oncologist from the Cancer Chemotherapy Center, Cancer Institute in Tokyo, has been a regular invited participant in the NCI Phase I and II meetings to exchange information on clinical protocols, procedures, and evaluation of clinical trials on new anticancer agents under investigation in Japan. He also visited the Northern California Oncology Group to discuss the final results of the US-Japan Cooperative Clinical Trial on Advanced Gastric Cancer during this visit.

A medical oncologist from the Cancer Institute, Tokyo, is spending one year in the Division of Cancer Treatment, NCI, to collaborate on studies on drug resistance in sublines of lung, breast, and ovarian cancer cells. He will also study the mechanism of the drug resistance and the effect and mechanism of calcium blockers.

In December 1983, a team of three American oncologists from the NCI and Memorial Sloan-Kettering Cancer Center visited several leading Japanese cancer centers and university hospitals to hold round-table discussions and seminars with their Japanese colleagues on the "Current Status of Chemotherapy for Curable Cancers." Subjects discussed at these meetings at different locales were small cell carcinoma, ovarian cancer, testicular cancer, breast and gastrointestinal tumors. The five-day visit and seminars provided excellent opportunities for both groups to discuss problems of mutual interest and to exchange the latest clinical information before a large number of Japanese oncologists.

Interdisciplinary Program Area

In March 1984, a conference on "Statistical Methods in Cancer Epidemiology" was held at the Radiation Effects Research Foundation (RERF) in Hiroshima. The organizers were Dr. Takeshi Hirayama, National Cancer Center Research, and Dr. William A. Blot, NCI. The participants included 9 Japanese and 10 American scientists, including 2 Americans who are currently on the RERF staff. In addition, some 20 Japanese biostatisticians, clinicians, and epidemiologists attended the two-day session to discuss the role of statisticians in cancer research; cancer mapping and disease clustering in Japan; case-control studies, including study of breast cancer among atomic bomb survivors; cohort studies; clinical studies and screening. The meeting was concluded on the subject of future directions for biostatistics and cancer epidemiology in Japan. There was very successful interaction among clinicians, statisticians and epidemiologists to discuss the roles played by specialists to advance the status of cancer epidemiology.

The workshop on "The Role of Pathologists in Epidemiology" was held in San Francisco in March 1984 in combination with the meeting of the International Academy of Pathology. In attendance were 7 Japanese and 7 American pathologists and epidemiologists who presented talks on autopsy registration in Japan, pathology of gastrointestinal tumors, geographic and etiologic differences in liver cancer, hormonal relation of breast cancer, racial differences in the incidence of prostate cancer, occupational aspects of lung cancer, geographic pathology, pathology of cancer in Japanese migrants in Hawaii, and T-cell lymphomas and other lymphatic diseases. This workshop enabled most of the participants to attend the full sessions at the meetings sponsored by the Academy during the following week.

In February 1984, a special meeting of the Joint NCI-JSPS Steering Committee was held in Tokyo to discuss the new 10-year Comprehensive Cancer Control Program, which had been announced by the Prime Minister of Japan in March 1983. The new program in Japan will begin in the fall of 1984 with most of the funds used to support basic and clinical cancer research in Japan. It was announced that international cooperation between the U.S. and Japan will be enhanced and expanded with the invitation of several imminent and young American scientists to study in Japan on short and long-term bases. The NCI-JSPS Steering Committee will be most willing to assist in developing and implementing the initiation of this new cancer program in Japan.

A pathologist from the Aichi Cancer Center in Nagoya, Japan, attended the 1983 Lymphoma Panel Meeting in Chicago to present his work on "T-cell Lymphomas in Japan." In addition, he visited the NCI, the Massachusetts General Hospital, and other research institutions to cooperate on studying and exchanging information on histologic findings and classification of various types of T-cell lymphomas.

A hematologist-pathologist from Tokyo University visited the University of Washington in Seattle to give a immunohistologic demonstration of surface markers on malignant lymphomas of T cell origin found in the U.S. and Japan. He also discussed plans for future collaboration between laboratories to study T-cell lymphomas.

An internist-oncologist from Tokyo University spent three weeks at the University of Southern California in Los Angeles to discuss methods of early detection of hepatocarcinoma using tumor markers, such as AFP, CEA, and others. They also discussed the differences in liver cancer among the Japanese and American population.

In totality, the past year has been very productive for exchange of information and an excellent group of scientific personnel.

COOPERATION WITH POLAND

In spite of the current political situation in Poland, the exchange of scientists from Poland, under the US-Poland Cancer Program, has not greatly diminished.

During this fiscal year, a Polish pathologist from the Institute of Oncology in Gliwice spent three months in the Department of Pathology, Memorial Sloan-Kettering Cancer Center in New York, to become acquainted with the latest, modern trends in tumor pathology. He took special training in tumor pathology, studied the organization of a well designed pathology department, learned the new procedures in immunohistochemistry, production of monoclonal antibodies for tumor diagnosis, and the screening procedures for early detection of neoplasia of the respiratory tract, urinary tract, and the female genital tract. He also visited other laboratories in the New York area and in Philadelphia to meet with and discuss problems of mutual interest with the respective staff members.

In November 1983, a young radiology technician from the Institute of Oncology in Warsaw who arrived at the Radiological Physics Laboratory at the University of Texas System Cancer Center in Houston, to spend eight months participating in an intensive course in principles and calibration of interstitial and intercavity dosimetry, high energy electron, and neutron dosimetry. She also observed and learned the latest techniques used in the Radiotherapy Clinic in order to make comparison of methods used in the Institute in Warsaw. She attended many lectures presented by the senior staff at the Cancer Center. She also visited the Presbyterian-St. Luke Hospital in Chicago and the Memorial Sloan-Kettering Cancer Center before returning to Poland.

A woman radiotherapist from the Institute of Oncology in Warsaw spent six months in the Department of Radiotherapy, the University of Texas System Cancer Center, to study interstitial and intracavity dosimetry, observed and discussed the latest methods in radiological treatment of tumor, and gained laboratory experience in the radiobiology of tumor and normal tissues. She also spent an extra month at the Memorial Sloan-Kettering Cancer Center to meet and discuss latest methodologies in radiation oncology with the senior staff members.

COOPERATION WITH FRANCE

During this fiscal year, the NCI and the French National Institute for Health and Medical Research (INSERM) agreed to continue the US-France Cancer Program for another three years with a slight modification of the program structure. It was agreed that the two program areas, the Basic Cancer Research and the Clinical Cancer Research Program Areas, be abolished and that there would be one central steering committee for each agency to nominate and approve applicants for exchange scientist appointments in all areas of cancer research. In addition, members of either steering committee are able to propose scientific seminars or workshops on specific topics of mutual interest. The bilateral program has put emphasis on exchange of scientific personnel and to refrain from holding large review meetings in the future. A special joint committee will be held only when policy decisions have to be discussed.

In FY 1984 a biochemist from the Laboratory of Pharmacokinetics, Marseille, France, undertook a long-term advanced training in biochemical pharmacology at the Grace Cancer Drug Center, Roswell Park Memorial Institute in Buffalo, New York. She has been studying the determinants of response to antimetabolites, using Ara-C in preclinical model systems, including in vivo and in vitro sensitive and resistant cells to Ara-C, as well as P-388 tumor cells. She also studied the methods for the assay of drug metabolism, using cell cultures, high performance liquid chromatography, radioimmunoassay, enzyme and precursor inhibitor assays.

A physiologist from the INSERM Laboratory and the Faculty of Pharmacy in Marseilles has spent one year in the Divisions of Medical Oncology and Biochemical Pharmacology, Medical College of Virginia in Richmond, studying the cellular pharmacology of the 7-hydroxy derivative of methotrexate in ascites tumor cells. In addition, he has been studying the interaction between 7-hydroxy methotrexate and methotrexate at the level of cell transport carrier and polylpolyglutamate synthetase. His training will be valuable in maintaining the collaborative activities between the laboratories in Marseilles and Richmond.

A pharmaceutical scientist from the Institut Gustave-Roussy, Villejuif, France, studied at the Gastrointestinal Unit of the Massachusetts General Hospital in Boston for six months. He collaborated in the in vitro and in vivo studies of monoclonal antibodies for the early detection and therapy of hepatocellular carcinoma. His research was focused on the cytotoxic activity of monoclonal antibodies against alphafetoprotein and against hepatocellular carcinoma associated antigens. He also studied a cytotoxicity model system using immunotherapy and immunotargeted drug chemotherapy.

A pharmacologist from the Institut Curie-Biologie, Centre Universitaire, Orsay, studied in the Department of Pharmacology, Harvard Medical School in Boston, for a period of six months collaborating on DNA synthesis by DNA polymerase, enzymatic digestion of DNA, high performance liquid chromatography of products resulting from DNA degradation by activated neocarzinostatin, analysis of base release, and the use of radiolabelled DNA. The methodologies will be applied to ongoing studies at his home institution to study the mode of action of new analogues of cancer drugs and in vivo studies of the effect of anticancer drugs on animal tumors by nuclear magnetic resonance.

A microbiologist from the Laboratory of Viral Oncology, Institut de Recherches

Scientifiques sur le Cancer, Villejuif, studied the biochemical effect of interferon on murine macrophages at the Laboratory of Cellular Physiology, Rockefeller University in New York. Upon his return to his home laboratory, active collaboration between the two laboratories will be continued to study the function of macrophages, as well as other forms of interferon and lymphokines.

A hematologist from the University of North Carolina, Chapel Hill, studied for six months at the INSERM Unit, Institut de Pathologie Cellulaire, Hopital de Bicetre, Bicetre, to collaborate on the problem of proliferation and maturation of human myeloid leukemia, as well as share the latest advances in flow cytometry and measurements of cell cycle kinetics. It is anticipated that the two laboratories will continue the cooperation in the future.

In FY 1985 a workshop on "Bone Marrow Transplantation" is being planned to be held in Bethesda with leading experts from both countries to present their latest research.

COOPERATION WITH EGYPT

Scientists and clinicians of the National Cancer Institute of Cairo University have been collaborating with counterpart specialists at the National Cancer Institute on a Phase II study of chemotherapy of urinary bladder cancer, breast cancer, and other types of cancer. This cooperative project was initiated in 1976 between the two institutions and has been supported under the Special Foreign Currency Program (PL 480). This project continues to be the mainstay of the cooperation in cancer research.

A collaborative project on the "Epidemiologic and Clinical Studies of Lymphomas and Leukemias" was initiated this past year between the National Cancer Institute and the Cairo Cancer Institute. This project has been progressing satisfactorily with the cooperation of the International Agency for Research on Cancer in Lyon, France.

As a corollary to the cooperative project on lymphomas and leukemias, a senior pathologist-cytogeneticist from the Department of Pathology, Cairo Cancer Institute, visited the National Cancer Institute for a period of two weeks to confer on the progress of the research project and also learned some of the new techniques of karyotyping of lymphoma and leukemia cells. He visited the Department of Human Genetics, Johns Hopkins University, Baltimore, Maryland, to discuss the collaborative studies on cytogenetics between the Cairo Cancer Institute and Johns Hopkins.

COOPERATION WITH THE FEDERAL REPUBLIC OF GERMANY

Under the Drug Development and Clinical Studies Program Area, a senior NCI investigator visited and spent one week in Germany to exchange information on new anticancer drugs and presented the latest information on the NCI preclinical antitumor drug testing program. He also discussed present collaborative efforts and future plans for cooperation in screening and testing new drugs. During the trip, he visited the Institute of Chemistry and Pharmaceutical Science, University of Regensburg; the West German Tumor Center, Essen; the Medical Clinic of Freiburg University; and the Department of Toxicology and Chemotherapy, German Cancer Research Center in Heidelberg. He also attended the annual symposium on chemotherapy sponsored by the NCI and the European

Organization for Research on the Treatment of Cancer in Brussels, Belgium.

In the Environmental Carcinogenesis Program Area there has been a meeting of the Program Coordinators to revamp the research areas to be covered. It has been tentatively agreed that in addition to environmental carcinogenesis, cell biology, immunology, and viral oncology would be included to provide coverage of basic cancer research.

COOPERATION WITH CHINA (MAINLAND)

Four Chinese scientists attended a joint US-Chinese workshop on the Epidemiology of Cancer, which was held in Honolulu during the month of January.

A feasibility study was successfully completed for a nutrition intervention study of esophageal cancer in Linxian, a county which has the highest rates of esophageal cancer in the world. Full-scale trials are expected to begin in the fall of 1984. Subjects in this study will receive various combinations of vitamins (retinol, beta-carotene, riboflavin, niacin, vitamin C, vitamin D, and vitamin E) and minerals (molybdenum, selenium, and zinc). This study is funded by NCI contract N-CP2-1012.

The three following projects are also in an early phase of data collection: esophageal and liver carcinogenesis and biochemical epidemiology (two projects); and an interdisciplinary study on leukemia and lymphoma. Studies will be conducted in Chinese populations at high risk of developing esophageal or liver cancer, using immunologic and biochemical probes for different carcinogens. Monoclonal antibodies will be utilized to measure exposure, metabolism, and DNA damage by the carcinogens in high risk populations. The Chinese will provide human (primarily fetal) esophageal explants and epithelial cells for one study and human liver samples for the other, which will be used for joint analysis. Initial results have shown that human liver and esophageal tissues and cells can be maintained in culture. Studies of carcinogen metabolism have shown that cultured tissues and cells can activate several different classes of environmentally important carcinogens. The third project is a pilot study on the epidemiology of leukemia and lymphoma in China, in which epidemiologic, immunopathologic, virologic, and treatment hypotheses will be tested in an attempt to characterize the features of a type of T-cell lymphoma caused by human T-cell leukemia lymphoma virus (HTLV).

COOPERATION WITH ITALY

Bilateral activities in Cancer Prevention and Cancer Therapeutics constitute broad efforts in the collaboration between American and Italian cancer specialists.

Under the Prevention Program Area an epidemiologist from the National Institute of Occupational Safety and Health, Cincinnati, was invited to present a paper on "Epidemiologic Study of Employees in a Leather Tannery" at the Congress of Tannery Workers, which was held in Italy in November 1983. He visited the Center for the Study and Prevention of Cancer in Florence and presented a talk on "Occupational Safety and Health in the U.S." He also visited the National Institute for Research on Cancer in Genova to discuss problems of mutual interest on occupational safety and health. It is anticipated that the visits to the Italian laboratories will result in future collaborations.

In May 1984 the workshop on "Epidemiology of Childhood Cancer" was held at the Villa Durazzo, Santa Margharita Ligure, Italy. Topics discussed at the workshop included the epidemiological overview of childhood cancer with emphasis on environmental risk factors, recent developments in the genetics of childhood cancer in Italy, ongoing studies in epidemiology in Italy and the U.S., multi-center clinical cooperative efforts in Italy, late mortality and second cancers, and other subjects of mutual interest. Also, the joint American-Italian group met to discuss the ongoing cooperative case-control study of stomach cancer, which has a high incidence in northern Italy. Discussions were also held on collaboration on carcinogenesis research.

The Joint Cancer Therapuetics Committee held a review meeting in Bethesda in October 1983 in conjunction with workshops on the "Mechanism of Cancer Cell Metastases and Effects of Drugs" and "The Use of Monoclonal Antibodies in Tumor Therapy." Following the workshops, the Steering Committee held a brief meeting to discuss the status of collaborative programs on breast cancer, pediatric oncology, clinical biochemical pharmacology, and biological response modifiers. The Committee also discussed and planned the strategies for future meetings and the exchange of personnel.

During the year, a young Italian oncologist from the Laboratory of Clinical Pharmacology, Istituto de Ricerche Farmacologiche "Mario Negri," Milan, continued his training at the Harvard School of Public Health in Boston to study cancer management practices and to obtain further training in epidemiology and bio-statistics. The experience gained at Harvard will assist him in planning a program for the evaluation of diagnosis and therapy procedures in a number of general and community hospitals in Italy. He will also be involved with the Italian National Breast Cancer Task Force studies.

A medical oncologist from the Centro de Endocrinologia ed Oncologia Esperimentale, Naples, joined the Medicine Branch, Division of Cancer Treatment, NCI, for a period of one year to collaborate on the studies of immunotherapy of lymphoid neoplasms.

A pediatrician from the Istituto Giannina Gaslini in Genova, spent 2 months in the Pediatric Oncology Branch, NCI, to observe and learn the treatment methods for autologous bone marrow infusion in children with cancer. The Italian institute is developing a clinical unit for bone marrow treatment in order to collaborate with the NCI program.

A pharmacologist from the Istituto Nazionale per la Ricerce sul Cancro, Genova, is spending a year at the Grace Cancer Drug Center, Roswell Park Memorial Institute, Buffalo, to study the biochemical and pharmacological basis for the selective in vivo action of anticancer agents. Studies will use 5-fluorouracil and 5'deoxyfluorouridine as models in normal and tumor bearing animals. In vitro studies will also be conducted with human cell cultures to study the metabolism of anticancer drugs.

A pediatrician from the Catholic University of Rome, collaborated with senior investigators for three weeks in the Pediatric Oncology Branch, NCI, on the study of clinical pharmacology of oral 6-mercaptopurine and serial computerized tomography scan studies in children with acute lymphoblastic leukemia. These studies are part of the ongoing collaborative effort in pediatric oncology between the Catholic University and the NCI.

In May 1984, the National Research Council of Italy approved and announced the new 5-year Program of Cancer Research. At the current rate of monetary exchange, 110 billion lira is equivalent to 70 million U.S. dollars.

The program will involve some 500 researchers and the coordinator will be Professor Umberto Veronesi, Director of the National Cancer Institute in Milano. The new program will be broadly based including clinical research on various types of cancer and basic laboratory research related to molecular biology, cell biology, immunology, and pharmacology.

COOPERATION WITH HUNGARY

Cooperation was established between the Uniformed Services University of the Health Sciences (USUHS) in Bethesda and the Institute of Oncopathology in Budapest for the study of familial cancer. This program involves the exchange of personnel and tissue samples. One guest worker from Hungary is currently working at USUHS under this program.

A U.S. pathologist visited four institutes in November 1983 for the purpose of initiating collaborative clinical studies and experimental investigations related to cellular immunity, the effects of interferon, and cancer. As a result of this visit, a protocol was developed for analysis of blood samples from Hungarian males at risk for acquired immune deficiency syndrome (AIDS).

A follow-up visit to Budapest was made in August 1984 by this same pathologist. During this time he worked with staff members at the State Institute of Dermatology-Venerology to collect tissue samples from patients with AIDS, Kaposi's sarcoma, and autoimmune diseases including systemic lupus erythrematosus. These tissue samples will be subsequently studied for cytopathologic changes in lymphocytes and vascular endothelium which have been associated with tumor development, interferon stimulation, and hepatitis virus infection. During this same visit, arrangements were made for a collaborative study of lymphocytic thymomas using labeled monoclonal antibodies. Relatively little work has been done in this area, and the frequency of thymoma is high in Hungary.

In February 1984, an NCI pathologist visited the National Institute of Oncology and the First Institute of Pathology in Budapest to continue ongoing collaboration in the following areas: 1) aging processes in breast cancer; 2) evaluation of data processing systems in pathology; and 3) publication of a book chapter titled "Incipient Neoplastic Lesions in the Liver." During this visit arrangements were made to test antibodies directed against breast cancer tissue. These tests are to be conducted in the United States later this year.

Based upon prior discussions, the Hungarians have developed a system for coding and processing pathology diagnostic statements. The system is now operational and plans are being made to include several other hospitals within the computer network.

An NCI medical oncologist visited the National Institute of Oncology in April to investigate the possibility of establishing cooperative clinical programs between this and other institutes in Hungary with NCI. During this visit, it was observed that there is a small anticancer drug development program in Hungary. At the present time the following compounds are in various stages of development:

dibromodulcitol, dianhydrogalactitol (DAG), diacetyl-DAG, disuccinyl-DAG, and a nitrosourea derivative. It is hoped that the National Institute of Oncology can become a resource for the NCI drug development program.

A scientist from the National Institute of Hematology and Blood Transfusion in Budapest came to NCI in October for a period of six months to develop a model for autologous killing by natural killer (NK) cells through the utilization of other traget cells, e.g. fibroblasts and autologous thymus cells, following cardiac surgery. Initial results have been encouraging, and it is expected that two publications will result from this study.

The Director of the First Institute of Pathology at the Semmelweis Medical University in Budapest visited six U.S. institutes during the month of October for the purpose of observing the priorities and thrusts of cancer research at these institutes and comparing them with those in Hungary.

A scientist from the National Institute of Hygiene in Budapest visited counterparts at laboratories of a pharmaceutical firm, NCI, and the Massachusetts Institute of Technology for the purpose of comparing results of studies on: 1) short and long-term toxic and genotoxic effects of environmental chemicals and 2) carcinogenicity of N-nitroso compounds.

A surgeon from the National Institute of Oncology arrived in October to spend ten months on several surgical services, with primary emphasis on breast surgery, at Roswell Memorial Park Institute. During this visit, he was able to observe the latest surgical techniques and procedures used in this country.

A pediatrician from the Semmelweis Medical University arrived in January to spend six months at the Children's Hospital Medical Center in Boston. During this period, he carried out studies on acute myelogenous leukemia and was exposed to some ongoing clinical studies in the management of children with pediatric oncologic problems.

COOPERATION WITH ROMANIA

An agreement was signed October 31, 1983, between NCI and the Victor Babes Institute in Bucharest. Cooperative research will be conducted in the areas of immunology, experimental pathology, molecular genetics, and clinical studies on diagnostic procedures. An initial visit was made in May by the NCI Scientific Coordinator to establish a plan for initial research efforts under the agreement.

In summary, the foregoing bilateral and multilateral scientific relationships between the NCI and its counterpart foreign institutions/organizations are indicative of significant contributions to the overall international health policy of the United States. Cancer is a global health problem and forces us to look beyond our national borders and concerns. Cancer still is beyond the remedial powers of any single country and, as collaboration in health becomes an even greater responsibility of the world citizenship, it is important that we continue to direct our international cancer activities so that they respond to specific differences among countries and to be assured that there is return benefit to the people of the United States.

III. ACTIVITIES WITH INTERNATIONAL ORGANIZATIONS

A CLEARINGHOUSE FOR ONGOING RESEARCH IN CANCER EPIDEMIOLOGY is a cooperative project supported jointly by the International Cancer Research Data Bank (ICRDB) Section, the International Agency for Research on Cancer (IARC) in Lyon, France, and the German Cancer Research Center in Heidelberg. The CLEARINGHOUSE, located in Lyon, collects, processes, and disseminates detailed data on research to cancer epidemiology and studies related to the cause of cancer in countries throughout the world. The CLEARINGHOUSE also prepares lists of epidemiology researchers and resources, responds to inquiries of a technical nature, and produces an annual Directory of Ongoing Research in Cancer Epidemiology.

The LATIN AMERICAN RESEARCH INFORMATION PROJECT (LACRIP) was developed through the ICRDB Program in collaboration with the Pan American Health Organization (PAHO) and its Regional Library of Medicine (BIREME) in Sao Paulo, Brazil. LACRIP serves as the source for identifying and collecting Latin American biomedical literature, summaries of ongoing cancer-related research projects, and active cancer therapy protocols in Latin America for inclusion in the CANCERLINE System. PAHO also serves as the center for searching ICRDB databases and providing documents and data in response to requests for information from cancer researchers in Latin America. A cancer literature update service is provided quarterly to cancer researchers and clinicians in Latin America.

In cooperation with the International Union Against Cancer (UICC), the ICRDB Section provides partial support for a special COMMITTEE FOR INTERNATIONAL COLLABORATIVE ACTIVITIES (CICA) within the framework of the UICC. One of the CICA activities is the collection of data on ongoing cancer research projects, including clinical protocols, from more than 70 countries. CICA personnel identify and promote collaborative projects among cancer centers and cancer scientists in different countries. CICA periodically publishes an updated International Directory of Specialized Cancer Research and Treatment Establishments, which describes more than 700 of the world's cancer centers and their cancer research and treatment activities and resources. An International Cancer Patient Data Exchange System (ICPDES) has been established as part of the CICA project. Currently, ICPDES participants include scientists and clinicians from nine European and five American cancer centers. This pilot project could result in the development and establishment of an internationally recognized information resource form which comparative data of value would be provided on cancer epidermiology, treatment, and prevention. Data is entered for all cancer types from each participating cancer center. Data for this activity has been collected since November 1977.

Scientist-to-Scientist Communication

The ICRDB Program, through the UICC in Geneva, Switzerland, encourages INTERNATIONAL SCIENTIST-TO-SCIENTIST COMMUNICATION through the UICC-administered International Cancer Research Technology Program (ICRETT). The goal of this program is the promotion of direct and rapid transfer of information about new or improved technology or methodology between two or more investigators, located in different countries and working on similar research projects. This interaction between such scientists is accomplished by the support of short-term visits for the purpose of conducting collaborative research projects over a brief interval of time, usually two to four weeks. Since the inception of the program in 1975 through March 1984, 720 ICRETT awards have been granted to scientists of 50 countries (Tables 1 and 2).

In many instances, ICRETT associations between scientists from different countries developed into significant collaborative studies that otherwise might not have acquired the impetus and the resources with which to evolve. Examples of such activities will follow.

A Belgian radiotherapist went to the University of Texas System Cancer Center in Houston to learn techniques to measure the effect of ionizing radiation on model systems of the lung, intestine, and tumor cells. A joint project, using mouse fibrosarcoma, was accomplished to assess the kinetics of cell repair, the influence of treatment protraction, and the distribution of irradiation on the magnitude of repopulation.

A biochemist from Thailand visited the Biochemical Institute, Freiburg University in Germany to study the tumor resistance developed during chemotherapy of liver cancer. Techniques learned in Germany will be valuable for developing similar investigations in Thailand.

A statistician from the University of Ibadan, Nigeria, visited the Birmingham and West Midlands Regional Cancer Registry in England to observe and learn the methods used in order to establish a computerized system in Nigeria for updating their cancer registry.

A cell biologist from Scotland studied the activation of oncogenes during multistage carcinogenesis in the Division of Radiation Biology, University of Arizona.

An Italian medial oncologist from Pavia visited the Division of Oncology, Stanford University School of Medicine, to observe and discuss the establishment of a full schedule program for therapy of lymphoma. He learned about the ongoing clinical trials on Hodgkin's disease and non-Hodgkin's lymphoma, evaluation of gonadal status of patients undergoing chemotherapy and prevention of sterility, the assessment of leukemogenic risk of combined modality treatment, and new perspectives in the therapy of non-Hodgkin's lymphoma using monoclonal antibodies and interferon.

A Czech biologist studied at the Wenner-Gren Institute in Stockholm, Sweden, to learn the technology or purification of T cell growth factor by fast protein liquid chromatography, which has been developed at the host laboratory.

An oncologist from the Philippines studied at the Aichi Cancer Center in Nagoya, Japan, to learn the methods for immunocytohistochemical characterization of lymphomas. She learned to use the peroxidase-antiperoxidose method to characterize lymphoma cells.

A Japanese pathologist visited the Tufts University Cancer Research Center in Boston to learn the latest technology using the fluorescence activated cell sorter to analyze, sort lymphocytes, and characterize the lymphostromal complex forming cells in normal thymus cells and preleukemic thymic lymphocytes.

Table 1. Summary from 1976 through March 31, 1984

Origin of ICRETT Awardees	
Argentina	19
Australia	4
Austria	7
Belgium	15
Brazil	8
Bulgaria	3
Canada	15
China (Mainland)	7
Colombia	4
Czechoslovakia	9
Denmark	1
Egypt	1
El Salvador	1
Finland	8
France	49
Germany (F.R.)	33
Greece	5
Hungary	4
India	26
Iran	3
Ireland	1
Israel	59
Italy	51
Japan	16
Kenya	2
Liberia	2
Malaysia	2
Mexico	4
Netherlands	13
New Zealand	2
Nigeria	8
Norway	15
Peru	1
Philippines	3
Poland	16
South Africa	2
Spain	4
Sri Lanka	3
Sweden	29
Switzerland	7
Taiwan	2
Thailand	4
Turkey	1
Uganda	1
United Kingdom	81
Uruguay	4
United States	157
Venezuela	1
Yugoslavia	6
Zambia	1
	720

Destination of ICRETT Awardees	
Argentina	1
Australia	11
Austria	1
Belgium	8
Brazil	1
Canada	14
China (Mainland)	9
Colombia	1
Denmark	8
Finland	8
France	46
Germany (F.R.)	39
Hungary	2
Iceland	1
India	4
Israel	10
Italy	10
Japan	28
Malaysia	1
Mexico	1
Netherlands	16
New Zealand	4
Norway	4
Peru	1
Poland	1
Soviet Union	3
Sweden	41
Switzerland	31
Taiwan	1
United Kingdom	84
United States	327
Venezuela	2
Zambia	1
	720

Table 2. International Cancer Research Technology Transfer (ICRETT)

Disciplines	1976 six months	1977	1978	1979	1980 + JFM 81	1981 Apr 81 Mar 82	1982 Apr 82 Mar 83	1983 Apr 83 Mar 84	Total
a. Epidemiology, Biostatistics, and Cancer Registries	–	3	5	7	7	5	7	10	44
b. Biochemistry, Moleccular Biology, and Biophysics	5	14	14	11	11	7	11	7	80
c. Viral Carcinogenesis	7	13	10	9	11	6	10	10	76
d. Chemical Carcinogenesis	3	14	8	13	12	5	4	8	67
e. Cell Biology and Cell Genetics	1	15	11	8	19	14	7	7	82
f. Experimental Pathology (histopathology, cytology, and cytogenetics)	4	5	12	14	10	3	8	6	62
g. Immunology	5	19	25	31	33	11	8	7	139
h. Experimental Chemotherapy	6	3	2	9	2	2	2	1	27
i. Surgical Oncology	–	1	2	–	4	–	1	1	9
j. Clinical Chemotherapy and Endocrinology	2	3	1	8	7	3	1	6	31
k. Radiobiology and Radiotherapy	5	4	7	10	9	7	10	4	56
l. Controlled Therapeutic Trials	1	–	1	4	–	–	2	1	9
m. Detection and Diagnosis	1	6	4	1	8	1	–	1	22
n. Behavioral and Social Sciences	–	–	1	–	4	1	3	1	10
o. Environmental Factors and Prevention	–	2	–	1	2	–	1	–	6
	40	102	103	126	139	65	75	70	720

IV. SPECIAL INFORMATION ACTIVITIES OF THE OFFICE OF INTERNATIONAL AFFAIRS

SCIENTIFIC INFORMATION BRANCH

The Scientific Information Branch (SIB), was created as a new branch from organizational components within the NCI in 1983 to optimize the information dissemination activities of the Institute. The branch is a component of the Office of International Affairs (OIA), Office of the Director (OD), of the National Cancer Institute (NCI) and is located in the the newly acquired R. A. Bloch International Cancer Information Center. The SIB consists of the Office of the Chief, and four sections: Cancer Treatment Reports (CTR); the Journal of the National Cancer Institute (JNCI); Literature Research (LR), and the International Cancer Research Data Bank (ICRDB). The Branch Chief has served as Acting Section Head of the ICRDB. The SIB plans, directs, coordinates, and evaluates the activities and operations of all of the NCI's scientific journals, its monographs, the specialized publications of the ICRDB, and on-line computerized databases that constitute the Institute's centralized information services. These services are targeted toward meeting the informational needs of basic scientists and clinical investigators.

A significant responsibility of the Branch this year has been the supervision of the development, implementation, and maintenance of the NCI's new on-line database, PDQ (Physician Data Query). The office of the chief, SIB, has had responsibility for coordinating the information gathering activities required for the development of this new, user-friendly, menu-driven database which has been developed by NCI with the cooperation of the National Library of Medicine (NLM). The PDQ system is accessible through the NLM's Medlars system. The PDQ database, described below, consists of three component files which are linked together for user-friendly retrieval through common data elements. All three files are organized to facilitate highly interactive and internally linked "user-friendly" search and retrieval, which can be accessed from a central computer by microprocessors using telecommunication systems such as Telenet and Tymnet. The system, which is updated on a monthly basis, was designed to be compatible with personal computers which are widely available commercially. The goal of PDQ is the dissemination of information on progress in cancer treatment to practicing physicians and the reduction of cancer mortality nationwide. To achieve these goals, the NCI is leasing the database to commercial vendors for nationwide distribution to physicians.

° The Cancer Information File contains prognostic and treatment information on 82 different types of cancer. For each tumor type a general summary (capsule statement) and a detailed summary (state-of-the-art statment) are provided describing current prognosis, definitions and explanations, staging, cellular classifications, treatment options that include a range of comparable standard therapies, and information on the investigational approaches under evaluation in clinical research trials, as well as key citations in the literature.

The file provides a convenient point of entry into the other two files which provide detailed information about physicians, treatment facilities and ongoing clinical trials. The prognostic and treatment information in the Cancer Information File was developed and refined in consultation with over 400 experts across the country who served as reviewers.

- The Directory File contains approximately 10,000 names, addresses, and telephone numbers of physicians who devote a major portion of their clinical practice to the treatment of cancer patients, and the names, addresses, and telephone numbers of 2,000 health-care institutions that provide care for cancer patients.

- The Protocol File contains over 1,000 active protocols supported by the National Cancer Institute as well as protocols submitted voluntarily by clinical investigators across the country. Each protocol summary provides study objectives, patient entry criteria, details of the treatment regimen and information about who is performing the trial and where it is being conducted. The Protocol File can also be searched for details about the treatment regimens, special study parameters, and treatment schedules.

An Editorial Board comprised of prominent medical, surgical, pediatric, and radiation oncologists is maintaining the currency and accuracy of the medical information in the PDQ Cancer Information File and recommending changes as new data becomes available. The PDQ Editorial Board is also responsible for reviewing protocols that have been submitted for inclusion in the PDQ database by clinical investigators who are not funded by NCI. The PDQ Editorial Board consists of 21 physicians, 13 from the Philadelphia, Baltimore, Washington, and Richmond areas, and 8 NCI staff. The Board monitors the literature and examines promising new treatment developments in cancer therapy, bringing significant advances to the attention of the full board for consideration.

An Associate Editorial Board consisting of 51 prominent physicians from the extramural community, nominated by the major professional oncologic societies, has been formed to serve as consultants to the PDQ Editorial Board.

The PDQ database became available through the National Library of Medicine's MEDLARS system in March, 1984. Negotiations with commercial software vendors interested in leasing PDQ are in progress. Plans for the upcoming year include optimization of the current files, the development and implementation of a drug file and a literature file, and the implementation of an office automation system that will improve the Branch's ability to provide the scientific and medical community with accurate and up to date information on advances in cancer research.

Cancer Treatment Reports Section

The Cancer Treatment Reports Section publishes Cancer Treatment Reports (CTR) and Cancer Treatment Symposia (CTS), two journals containing highly technical articles describing scientific research in all phases of clinical and preclinical cancer therapy. CTR is issued monthly and CTS is issued up to six times per year. CTR has a distribution of almost 8,000, which includes members of the local national, and international scientific communities as well as medical and university libraries. The Cancer Treatment Reports Section accomplishes the timely and accurate publication of these journals by processing (logging in, tracking the review and evaluation process, and maintaining status and decision files/correspondence) all submissions; by editing, designing, formatting, and proofreading all accepted articles; and by closely supervising and tracking the activities of the Government Printing Office (GPO) contractor in the final printing and distribution of each journal.

Cancer Treatment Reports

CTR was first printed in January of 1959 as Cancer Chemotherapy Reports under the direction of the Cancer Chemotherapy National Service Center program. From 1959 to 1968 the journal was issued 6-10 times a year, depending on the number of manuscripts submitted and accepted for publication. In 1968 the journal was expanded to three distinct parts:

Part 1: Original research, both experimental and clinical;

Part 2: Comprehensive, chemotherapy studies involving tabular material; and

Part 3: Program information including treatment protocols, clinical brochures, toxicology reports, and review articles.

In January 1976, the journal was renamed Cancer Treatment Reports. The three-part, separately numbered system was dropped and the journal began monthly publication. The journal was published by the Publications Section of the Division of Cancer Treatment (DCT) until October of 1983, when the section became known as the Cancer Treatment Reports Section of the expanded Scientific Information Branch (SIB) which was reorganized to the Office of International Affairs, Office of the Director, National Cancer Institute (NCI).

The journal now considers unsolicited and previously unpublished manuscripts of original research under six major categories:

1. Full length manuscripts (includes Current Controversies, Special Features, and Guest Editorials)
2. Brief Reports
3. Letters to the Editor
4. Clinical Trials Summaries
5. Meeting Reports
6. Mini-symposia

Special 25th Anniversary Issue:

In January 1984, CTR marked its 25th anniversary with the publication of a special issue which featured articles examining past progress and current expectations in cancer therapy. This issue includes articles by leaders in the fields of surgery, radiotherapy, and medical oncology, which trace the remarkable accomplishments of cancer treatment research over the past 35 years and look to the future for promising new approaches to cancer treatment. The issue examines the potential important new concepts such as monoclonal antibodies, interferon, hyperthermia, and neutron therapy, as well as more traditional subjects such as drug discovery and development.

An unprecedented 10,500 copies of this issue were printed and distributed: 8,500 in the first printing and another 2,000 in a second printing (as a result of a promotional "Special Communication" which generated the need for a second printing to accommodate the requests).

Editorial Board:

The Editorial Board of CTR includes the Editor-in-Chief and 12 associate editors. Dr. Robert E. Wittes, Associate Director, Cancer Therapy Evaluation Program, DCT, NCI, is the current Editor-in-Chief. Each year three editors rotate off the board and three new members are added. Provisions have been made to allow editors to have an additional year on the board at the discretion of the Editor-in-Chief and the Director, DCT. An Advisory Board of 15 members has also been established to supplement the areas of expertise represented by the associate editors (during 1984 these members will be changed because their two-year period of service is completed). The official policies of the journal are contained in a charter which was established in 1975.

All material submitted for consideration by CTR is subject to review by two or more outside referees and a member of the editorial board. The editorial board is responsible for determining the scientific content of the journal. The associate editors assign new manuscripts to reviewers and make decisions on the fate of each manuscript after review. Proposals for the publication of special Cancer Treatment Symposia (CTS) issues are discussed with the board by the Editor-in-Chief prior to formulation of a decision to publish. The board advises the Editor-in-Chief and the Managing Editor about scientific and administrative aspects of journal policy. In order to perform these tasks, the CTR editorial board meets regularly once a month.

Manuscript Submissions in 1983-1984:

During 1983, the editorial office processed 585 manuscript submissions, and so far in 1984 (May), 250 manuscripts have been submitted to CTR for consideration. To help in the tracking of the procedures involved in manuscript review we hope to implement a completely computerized document control system in the editorial office in 1984. By computerizing the system, we will be able to handle manuscript tracking tasks more efficiently and expeditiously and will be prepared if there is a conversion to electronic publishing in the near future by the Government Printing Office.

Table 3 shows a comparative analysis of publication activity over the last ten years.

Table 3*

	No. of manuscripts--		No. of--		
Year	Received	Accepted	Issues	Pages	Reviewers
1973	244	207		1100	167
1974	286	180	11	1823	213
1975	365	261	9	1888	295
1976	478	302	12	2021	402
1977	422	313	9	1771	432
1978	578	364	12	2168	557
1979	740	667	10	2175	695
1980	576	269	4	827	595
1981	499	212	6	1159	339
1982	572	282	12	2149	470
1983	585	333	11	1181	536
1984	250	105	5	824	--

*Does not include CTS.

As of May 15, 1984.

Sections of the Journal:

Full length manuscripts -- This section contains the results of clinical or pre-clinical research which have been given a high priority for publication as full-length manuscripts ranging from 7 to 20 printed pages. Included in this this section are special features, guest editorials, and commentaries from scientists (at the invitation of the editorial board) on subjects of current interest in cancer treatment. Also included in the full length section are the Current Controversies in Cancer Management articles which address the controversial aspects of cancer treatment.

Brief Reports -- This section contains short clinical manuscripts and abbreviated reports of preliminary research which can be processed more quickly than full-length manuscripts. They are cost efficient and serve to increase the number of current research studies which can be disseminated to the readership.

Clinical Trials Summaries -- This popular section contains concise summaries of data from clinical trials that have produced negative results. The format requires authors to limit their text to approximately 300 words and to summarize the tabular data into one table which lists patient characteristics, toxicity, response, and survival information. As with the Brief Reports section, the brevity of these reports allows for many to be edited and printed in each issue, resulting in rapid dissemination of that information. An annual table is compiled by the editorial office which summarizes the year's clinical trial summaries.

Letters to the Editor -- Letters to the editor may or may not be in response to previously published articles and are reviewed prior to acceptance as are any other manuscript submissions.

Meeting Reports and Mini-symposia -- When time and space permit, CTR publishes the proceedings of meetings (usually there are less than ten papers involved). The following were two symposia that appeared in CTR in 1983:

1. Workshop on Small Cell Anaplastic Carcinoma of the Lung. Cancer Treat Rep 67(1):1-43, 1983.

2. Symposium on Cellular Resistance to Anticancer Drugs. Cancer Treat Rep 67(10):855-923, 1983.

Miscellaneous -- CTR also has an announcements section at the end of every issue which announces meetings, fellowships, and other items of interest to cancer researchers. As needed, special announcements (obituaries, dedications, etc.) appear before the contents page as necessary. Finally, annual indexes by subject and author and a list of the year's reviewers are prepared by the editorial office and published in the last issue of each year.

Cancer Treatment Symposia

The publication of Symposia as an intermittent supplement to CTR has been given general approval. Each issue of CTS is currently approved at the NIH level and it is hoped that in 1984 the Office of Management and Budget (OMB) will grant our request for approval on a continuing basis. There have been a total of four new symposia issues printed in 1983 and 1984:

1. Proceedings of the United States-Japan Meeting on Drug Development and Cancer Treatment Research. Cancer Treat Symp 1:1-117, 1983.

2. Proceedings of the Workshop on Patterns of Failure After Cancer Treatment. Cancer Treat Symp 2:1-313, 1983.

3. The Interdisciplinary Program for Radiation Oncology Research. Cancer Treat Symp 1:1-191, 1984.

4. Proceedings of the Workshop on 2'-Deoxycoformycin: Current Status and Future Directions. Cancer Treat Symp 2:1-109, 1984.

Office of Management and Budget Approval

As a result of a request for continuing approval of Cancer Treatment Reports in January 1983, CTR was given approval to publish until June 30, 1985. Requesting approval requires extensive documentation which defines the purpose and scope of the journal, a breakdown of costs and distribution, and a general justification for continuation of publication.

Distribution of CTR:

As part of the approval to publish, the OMB allows CTR to distribute 3,225 free copies to qualified medical groups, physicians, and libraries. Another 4,000 copies are sent to the Government Printing Office to distribute to paid subscribers. In January 1984, there was an increase of 600 new subscribers. We hope to further enhance this subscription base through new efforts in marketing the journals as part of SIB promotional initiatives. Table 4 shows the breakdown of the readership of CTR as reflected by the distribution.

Coverage of CTR in Current Contents and Related Publications:

Since 1967, CTR has been listed in Current Contents, Life Sciences. In 1973, CTR was included in a new publication of current titles in collaboration with Science, Engineering, Medical and Business Data, Ltd., Oxford, England. The Japan Medical Service, which publishes a supplement to its Index of Japanese Medical Periodicals listing foreign publications, also includes CTR. In 1964, CTR began sending copies of each issue to the Chemical Abstracts Service for abstracting and indexing of the chemical information. In 1980, CTR began to send advanced copies for abstracting and indexing purposes to the Franklin Institute in Philadelphia.

Table 4 (Distribution of CTR)

1. Official Use (distributed at no cost)	
a. Federal Government	
SIB copies (staff and display copies)	75
NIH employees	175
NCI contractors and grantees	733
FDA employees	17
VA employees	41
VA libraries and hospitals	79
PHS employees	10
Armed services (employees and libraries)	24
b. State agencies	9
c. Research institutes (including libraries)	477
d. Medical schools and universities (including libraries)	209
e. Hospitals (including libraries)	343
f. Special advisory groups	24
2. Other copies distributed at no cost	
a. Foreign investigators and institutions	597
b. Foreign libraries	199
c. Pharmaceutical and related industries	59
d. Individuals (such as medical practitioners)	254
	3325
3. Superintendent of Documents	
a. Paid subscriptions	4000
b. File copies	17
c. Depository libraries	469
	7811
4. CTR authors (complimentary reprints)	100
TOTAL	7911

Journal of the National Cancer Institute Section

Highlighting the activities during this period was the relocation of the JNCI staff to the newly renovated R. A. Bloch International Cancer Information Center, adjacent to the main campus of the National Institutes of Health. The JNCI editorial office became a section of the Scientific Information Branch, a component of the Office of International Affairs.

During the 12-month period, May 15, 1983 to May 14, 1984, the Board of Editors reviewed 587 manuscripts submitted for publication in JNCI. These manuscripts were from the following sources:

National Cancer Institute: 47 (22 accepted, 6 rejected, 19 pending)

Other research institutions: 540 (192 accepted, 115 rejected, 233 pending)

Of the 540 manuscripts received from sources outside the National Cancer Institute, 211 were from authors in other countries. Authors from 30 foreign countries (Table 5) submitted manuscripts for publication in JNCI. Nearly a third of the submittals were from Japan, and the countries of Australia, Canada, and the United Kingdom accounted for another third of the papers submitted.

A substantial increase was noted in the total number of pages published. The yearly total was 2,8[illegible] pages compared to 2,657 pages in the preceding year. Volume 71 (July-December 1983) contained 1,411 pages and volume 72 (January-June 1984) contained 1,472. In addition to regular manuscripts, the content of JNCI during this period included eight guest editorials, two meeting highlights, two special reports, and one historical note.

Typesetting, printing, and binding of JNCI are performed by the McFarland Company Company of Harrisburg, Pennsylvania, under a two-year contract through the Government Printing Office. This contract represents a significant improvement over the previous contract in that it incorporates a shorter publication schedule. The shorter schedule will enable manuscripts to be published within 90 days after acceptance. This compares to an average of 129 days under previous contracts.

Marketing efforts are being made to increase the JNCI subscriber base. The American Association for Cancer Research kindly provided us with a mailing list of their members, and a promotional package was mailed to nearly 4,000 potential subscribers. Promotion activities are also being made in conjunction with the Scientific Information Branch exhibits at professional and scientific meetings. To date, exhibits have appeared in Washington, DC, Arlington, VA, Buffalo, NY, Atlanta, GA, Toronto, Canada, and Denver, CO.

The high standards of editing and publishing maintained by JNCI continue to be recognized. In the annual publication competition sponsored by the Washington Chapter of the Society for Technical Communication, JNCI received an Award of Excellence in the category of complete periodicals. This was the second consecutive year that JNCI received the award, which is based on excellence in writing, editing, graphics, and their total integration into the publication.

NCI monograph activity during this period included the publishing of three monographs. Three others are in the manuscript stage of publication, while two were approved but no manuscripts have been received. Pending the final presentation of computer tapes for one monograph that is to be produced by Videocomp, numbers have not been assigned to those monographs not yet published. The status of each is as follows:

Published:

No. 63: Biological Reponse Modifiers: Subcommittee Report; September 1983

No. 64: Management Operations of the National Cancer Institute That Influence the Governance of Science; May 1984

No. 65: Use of Small Fish Species in Carcinogenicity Testing; May 1984

In manuscript stage:

Forty-five Years of Cancer Incidence in Connecticut (Videocomp)

Photobiologic, Toxicologic, and Pharmacologic Aspects of Psoralens

Selection, Follow-up, and Analysis in the Prospective Studies of the American Cancer Society: A Workshop

Manuscripts not received:

Fourth Symposium on Epidemiology and Cancer Registries in the Pacific Basin

Proceedings of the Vitamin A and Cancer Prevention Conference

The term contract arrangement with the McFarland Company through the Government Printing Office continues to be satisfactory. One monograph, No. 63, received an Award of Excellence in the books category of the Society for Technical Communications publication competition.

Table 5. Countries of Origin of Manuscripts Submitted to JNCI 1983-84

Australia	9	Italy	10
Austria		Japan	65
Belgium		Kenya	
Brazil		Korea	
Canada	29	Netherlands	8
China	3	New Zealand	1
Czechoslovakia	1	Norway	2
Denmark	4	Poland	2
England	22	Scotland	2
Finland	2	South Africa	1
Federal Republic of Germany	8	Sweden	
France	14	Switzerland	2
German Democratic Republic	1	United States	376
India	4	Venezuela	
Ireland	1	Wales	
Israel	6		

International Cancer Research Data Bank (ICRDB) Section

Introduction and Overview

Established by the National Cancer Act of 1971, the ICRDB Section of the SIB has developed a comprehensive range of technical information services and products that effectively disseminate cancer research information to scientists around the world. The major products of ICRDB activities are

1) Online computer databases comprising the CANCERLINE system which enable scientists to retrieve cancer information at some 3,000 locations within the United States and 12 other countries.

2) Two major series of publications (CANCERGRAMs and ONCOLOGY OVERVIEWS) containing abstracts of published cancer research results in special formats designed for easy use and quick reference.

3) Other specialized information collection, analysis, and dissemination activities.

CANCERLINE Databases

The five databases comprising the CANCERLINE System are CANCEREXPRESS/CANCERLIT (abstracts of the published literature); CANCERPROJ (descriptions of cancer research projects); CLINPROT (detailed summaries of investigational clinical protocols); and PDQ/Directory (elements of CLINPROT data linked to prognostic and therapeutic information about 82 different cancers and information about providers of cancer patient care).

All these files are mounted in the Medical Literature Analysis and Retrieval System (MEDLARS) of the National Library of Medicine. The CANCERLINE files are described in more detail below. Over the past year, ICRDB has continued to contribute to the development and implementation of the NCI's new database, PDQ (Physician Data Query), which contains cancer treatment information and will be described in the next section.

CANCERLIT is a comprehensive archival file of more than 400,000 bibliographic records with abstracts describing cancer research results published in biomedical journals, proceedings of scientific meetings, books, technical reports, and other documents since 1963. During FY 1983, CANCERLIT was growing at an annual rate of nearly 60,000 abstracts. Since 1980, all entries in CANCERLIT have been indexed with the Medical Subject Heading (MeSH) vocabulary of the National Library of Medicine. Users now have the option of using either MeSH terms or free text terms to retrieve data from the CANCERLIT database.

Because input processing steps are performed rapidly and the file is updated monthly, the CANCERLIT database provides scientists with an up-to-date and easily accessible source of information about the most recently published results of cancer research, as well as archival material.

CANCEREXPRESS is a sub-file of CANCERLIT and contains the same reference material and index terms. However, unlike CANCERLIT which provides comprehensive and archival information on a topic, CANCEREXPRESS meets the needs of users who want a current awareness database containing only recent information from quality journals. To provide this type of data, CANCEREXPRESS records are limited to abstracts and citations from a carefully selected list of approximately 400 journals selected for the quality of the papers that are published. To keep it current, only records entered into the CANCERLINE system during the most recent four months are included in CANCEREXPRESS.

CANCERPROJ contains descriptions of some 20,000 current cancer research projects, including about 5,000 descriptions of projects underway in 83 countries outside the United States. The foreign projects are collected with the help of an international network of data coordinators, including staff members of the International Union Against Cancer (UICC) who help to establish and maintain this network. A new contractor was selected in May 1984 to resume the collection and processing of data for this file.

CLINPROT provides worldwide access to information on new therapeutic approaches which are under evaluation for the treatment of cancer patients throughout various parts of the world. Data contained in CLINPROT include detailed summaries of some 4,000 investigational cancer therapy protocols, including about 1,500 active protocols and 2,500 completed protocols which are now closed to patient entry.

The PDQ1/Directory File which was added to the CANCERLINE System in July 1983 contains brief descriptions of some 1,000 active investigational protocols linked to files containing the names, addresses and telephone numbers of physicians who serve as institutional contacts at organizations where these protocols are being evaluated. This file permits users to locate institutions and physicians who specialize in cancer patient care in specified geographic areas. Information from this database was incorporated in a user-friendly version of this database (see next section).

PDQ (Physician Data Query)

A user-friendly version of PDQ (Physician Data Query), with three files (the Cancer Information file, the Directory file, and the Protocol file) linked together by common elements, became available on on the NLM computer system, using an INQUIRE database management system, on March 1, 1984. It was made available to over 2,000 MEDLARS code holders at medical libraries and other primary health care organizations in May 1984. The PDQ database is updated each month to keep the data current and accurate. New treatment options are incorporated as recommended by an Editorial Board composed of prominent oncologists from each of the major therapeutic disciplines.

Publications of the ICRDB Section

In addition to the databases, the ICRDB Section of SIB publishes two major series of publications called CANCERGRAMs and ONCOLOGY OVERVIEWS. These publications are described below:

> The CANCERGRAMs are a series of 66 monthly current awareness bulletins, each containing abstracts/citations referring to recently published articles and other documents describing cancer research results. More than 10,000 cancer researchers receive issues of those CANCERGRAMs containing updating information most directly related to their area of research each month.
>
> ONCOLOGY OVERVIEWS are retrospective bibliographies containing abstracts/citations referring to papers published during the past several years on key cancer research topics of high current interest to scientists. Recent OVERVIEWS deal with cell response to damaged DNA, gastrointestinal carcinogenesis, psychosocial aspects of cancer patient care, diagnosis and treatment of Kaposi's Sarcoma, and immunomodulation in cancer.

In addition, ICRDB publishes Recent Reviews in Carcinogenesis as an annual supplement to CANCERGRAMs. Each issue is a compilation of the abstracts of the 250-400 review articles published in the "Notice of Current Reviews" section of CANCERGRAMs in the carcinogenesis area during the 12 preceding months.

Special Activities supported by the ICRDB Section

CIDACS: Under contract with the NCI, three Cancer Information Dissemination and Analysis Centers (CIDACS) function as information resources in three broad areas of cancer research. They are the CIDAC for Diagnosis and Therapy at the M. D. Anderson Hospital and Tumor Institute, Houston; and the CIDACs for Carcinogenesis and the CIDAC for Cancer Virology, Immunology, and Biology located at the Franklin Research Center, Philadelphia. Each CIDAC is staffed by scientists and a network of expert cancer researcher consultants. These staff members provide the expertise required for the preparation of CANCERGRAMs and ONCOLOGY OVERVIEWS as well as for other CIDAC functions including CANCERLINE searching and scientific guidance to the ICRDB Section.

Literature Research Section

During the year, the Literature Research Section was transferred from the Division of Cancer Treatment to the Office of International Affairs in the Office of the Director, NCI. In addition to fulfilling information needs of the OIA, the Section continues to serve the Division of Cancer Treatment by providing information from the published literature on all aspects of the therapy of cancer. Data from the fields of chemotherapy, radiotherapy, surgery, immunotherapy, and the related chemical and biomedical disciplines are used by the staff in Decision Network review, meeting FDA requirements for IND filing, preparing clinical brochures and annual drug reports, and as background for evaluation of toxicological and clinical studies.

Literature Services

The Section received and filled more than 400 requests for information during the year. Responses were provided as comprehensive or selected bibliographies, computer print-outs, abstracts or copies of articles. Over 250 of the requests entailed manual literature searches supplemented by the various automated bibliographic systems such as Medline, Toxline, and Cancerline.

Clinical searches were done for such subjects as randomized trials in lymphomas, the treatment of neoplasms of various sites, correlation between Kaposi's sarcoma and AIDS, incidence of cancer and the pharmacokinetics of antineoplastic drugs in the elderly, and the toxicology of high-dose cytarabine and its use in acute leukemia. Bibliographies were prepared, or updated, for such compounds as hexamethylene-bisacetamide and other cell differentiators, didemnin B, triciribine, pibenzimol, fludarabine, amsacrine, dihydrolenperone, and phyllanthoside. Searches were also done for such diverse subjects as the ethics of Phase I trials, investigational drug accountability, cancer risks in women, drug interactions, risks to personnel handling anticancer agents, and animal models for bone marrow transplantation. A total of 55 bibliographies were prepared for compounds discussed at six Decision Network meetings.

References were also compiled for reports of Phase I studies with 43 agents for a project assessing therapeutic benefits in such trials. In an ongoing project, searches were completed for results of single agent Phase II studies with 33 drugs for use in the Cancer Therapy Evaluation Program Information System.

Support for the Physician Data Query system was provided by verification of citations prior to their input into the system, and by identification of original or updated references for specific regimens in the treatment of various neoplasms.

The Section serves all areas of the Institute, processing automated searches and providing assistance and instruction in the use of the Medlars system. Responses to more than 100 requests were in the form of computer print-outs only. Monthly SDI (Selective Dissemination of Information) bibliographies are produced for members of the staff on specific subjects of continuing interest.

A further responsibility of the Section is the maintenance of the Scientific Information Branch Library, a collection of journals and books for the use of NCI staff. Copies of over 70 journals are regularly received including many of the cancer journals, abstracting and indexing secondary sources, and chemical, biomedical or information science journals of special interest to the Section and other personnel in the building.

COMPUTER COMMUNICATIONS BRANCH

The Computer Communications Branch (CCB), was created in October 1983 and is located in the Office of International Affairs, OD, NCI. The CCB maintains and operates a computer center and its associated on-line terminal devices in support of centralized scientific and medical information services of the National Cancer Institute. Other activities include developing and publishing standards and procedures for use of the central facility and the remote devices linked to it; developing and acquiring systems software and telecommunications to support the central NCI facility; coordinating all hardware and systems software of the computer center to optimize efficient operation; developing, maintaining and upgrading by exploiting state-of-the-art technology, highly specialized electronic information delivery systems; and recommending plans and policies for improvement of centralized computer facilities to other NCI activities. CCB personnel include electronic engineers/technicians, program analysts, computer specialists/assistants, and a secretary.

The CCB is the organizational home for computer/production support of the Physician Data Query (PDQ) Program, a complex and far-ranging cancer knowledge base/information program designed to serve as a bridge between clinical researchers and practicing physicians for state-of-the-art information on cancer treatment methodologies and research protocols, see the International Cancer Research Data Bank (ICRDB) Section, Scientific Information Branch (SIB) for a description of PDQ. As such, PDQ makes use of expertise ranging from cancer specialists (the PDQ Editorial Board and the parallel PDQ Board of Associate Editors see the SIB) and users of varied backgrounds who are involved in PDQ from both the public and private sectors.

The CCB responsibility associated with PDQ is the monthly production of PDQ external tape output for the National Library of Medicine and other information vendors in the private sector. The information on the tapes is the culmination of data collection and input from several ICRDB Section contractors and a CCB contractor. It is categorized into the following files.

DESCRIPTION: An overview file describing PDQ and warning of restrictions on duplicating PDQ data.

CANCERINFO: A file consisting of an index of cancer diagnoses, a capsule summary describing each cancer, and state-of-the-art information about each cancer. The capsule summary consists of general prognostic information, stage explanations, and treatment options by stage. The state-of-the-art information describes the full range of treatment approaches available for each treatment modality for each stage and/or histologic subtype.

DIRECTORY: A file containing the list of physicians and organizations that specialize in cancer treatment.

PROTOCOL: A file that contains information on all cancer treatment protocols supported by NCI and all voluntarily submitted protocols from cancer organization/institutions throughout the United States as well as foreign countries. Active protocols (protocols open for patient entry), contain additional information on participating organizations/institutions and physicians.

CANCERTERM: A file that contains the names, synonyms, definitions, and interrelationships of the cancer terminology used in the PDQ knowledge base/information system.

Other CCB support is for the SIB journal sections, the Journal of the National Cancer Institute (JNCI) and Cancer Treatment Reports (CTR). Support is required for manuscript tracking and other informational activities associated with production of JNCI and CTR.

IV. OTHER NCI INTERNATIONAL PROGRAMS

The NIH Visiting Program

During 1984, scientists of the National Cancer Institute received scientists from 40 countries who came to the United States to engage in collaborative cancer research activities. There was a total of 276 foreign visiting scientists, associates, and fellows. Thirteen of the visitors were appointed as experts and 66 came as Guest Workers, whose financial support was provided by sources other than the NCI. The activities of these visiting scientists were pursued in the laboratories of the NCI's divisions of cancer treatment, cancer etiology, and cancer biology and diagnosis. These associations have been mutually beneficial. The NCI host scientists were afforded opportunities to learn from his/her visitor about cancer problems in a given foreign country; about factors peculiar to that nation that might be related to the morbidity and mortality of cancer; and about activities underway toward the management, treatment, and prevention of cancer. Reciprocally, the foreign visitors were provided with unique opportunities to improve their mastery of the scientific method or to develop their potential for significant contributions to basic and/or clinical research. The value and benefit of such scientific interaction can be assessed, ultimately, on the knowledge that cancer patients throughout the world are benefitting from an improved quality of care.

NCI-Sponsored Research in Foreign Countries

During 1984, the Divisions of Cancer Treatment, Cancer Etiology, Cancer Biology and Diagnosis, and Cancer Prevention and Control maintained extensions of their programmatic objectives in foreign countries through 18 contract research activities (Table 6).

The Division of Extramural Activities provided the fiscal support, through 45 grants and contracts, to scientists in foreign institutions conducting basic and applied cancer research (Table 6).

Institutions in 17 nations currently are the recipients of NCI grants and contracts. Thus, the outreach of NCI support extends to Australia, Belgium, Canada, China (Mainland), Denmark, Finland, France, Germany (FRG), Ghana, Israel, Italy, Jamaica, Japan, Sweden, Switzerland, Tanzania, and the United Kingdom.

Division of Cancer Biology and Diagnosis

In FY 1984, the Division of Cancer Biology and Diagnosis made 11 conference grants to support meetings and international conferences on tumor biology and immunology in the United States. At all the conferences, many leading foreign experts in tumor biology and immunology participated and presented their experimental work. Three of these scientific meetings were held as part of the annual Gordon Research Conference in the New England states.

Under the division's Immunology Program, ten research grants have been awarded to leading foreign laboratories. There are currently two grants awarded to scientists at the Karolinska Institute in Sweden and four grants to three institutions in Israel. Other grants have been awarded to laboratories in Australia, Finland, the United Kingdom, and the Federal Republic of Germany.

Table 6. NCI Grants and Contracts to Foreign Countries

Countries	No. Grants	$ Amount	No. Contracts	$ Amount	$ Totals
Australia	3	$ 149,034	-	-	$ 149,034
Belgium			1	$ 199,286	199,286
Canada	4	205,060	1	320,546	525,606
China (Mainland)	-		2	732,274	732,274
Denmark		184,512	-		184,512
Finland	2	100,501		1,268,000	1,368,501
Germany (FRG)		78,458	-		78,458
Ghana				28,500	28,500
Israel	8	621,506	1	137,500	759,006
Italy				200,000	200,000
Jamaica				200,000	200,000
Japan			2	281,000	281,000
Sweden	3	230,722	-		230,722
Tanzania				50,000	50,000
United Kingdom	3	180,179	3	693,129	873,308
International Organization			5	723,603	723,603
TOTALS	25	$1,749,972	20	$4,833,838	$6,583,810

The diagnostics program has awarded one grant each to the Tel Aviv University in Israel, the University of Copenhagen in Denmark, and the University of London, United Kingdom.

The tumor biology program has awarded two grants to the Walter and Eliza Hall Institute for Medical Research in Australia, one grant to the Ontario Cancer Treatment and Research Foundation in Canada, three grants to institutions in Israel, one grant to the University of Helsinki in Finland, and one grant to the Karolinska Institute in Sweden.

Senior staff of the division have particiapted in the areas of molecular biology, diagnostic research, experimental pathology, and cancer immunology with foreign scientists under the US-Japan Cooperative Cancer Research Program, the US-Poland Cancer Program, the US-France Cancer Program, and the US-Hungary Cancer Program.

Division of Cancer Etiology

The Division of Cancer Etiology (DCE) maintains active associations with international organizations and agencies that have well-defined objectives in cancer research, especially its cause, and basic studies on prevention. As well, DCE is engaged in collaborative contract research with eight institutions/agencies in eight foreign nations. These foreign extensions of the DCE research program thrusts enable the division to support fundamental studies on normal and malignant cells in relation to such carcinogens as viruses and chemicals, as well as epidemiologic studies of human populations for the identification of risk factors predisposing individuals to various cancers. Excellent model systems are available to scientists studying the effects of potentially carcinogenic factors in the environment. Thus, studies are related primarily to three major program areas within DCE: biological carcinogenesis, chemical and physical carcinogenesis, and epidemiology and biostatistics.

The binational programs in which DCE collaborates provide epidemiologic opportunities of significance to cancer research. This year special emphasis was given to joint studies and exchange programs with scientists of the Cancer Institute (Hospital) in Beijing to pursue clues drawn from the recent county-based maps in China (Mainland) and the changing risks among migrants to the United States. Reports were prepared on the geographic correlations within China (Mainland) between cancer of the cervix and penis, colorectal cancer and schistosomiasis, and on the patterns of childhood cancer in Chinese populations around the world. Collaborative analytic investigations are being developed in China (Mainland) on cancers of the esophagus, lung, stomach, and choriocarcinoma.

Through the mechanism of a contract with DCE, scientists at the Chaim-Sheba Medical Center in Israel are determining the incidence of cancer in 10,000 Israeli children exposed to radiotherapy for ringworm of the scalp, in 10,000 nonexposed persons selected from the general population, and in 5,000 nonexposed siblings. This effort is of significance in the study of patients irradiated for benign diseases in that it is an important area for evaluating biologic mechanisms for carcinogenesis in humans. The minimal confounding effects of carcinogenic influences and the possible greater susceptibility of young people to environmental carcinogens, enhance the chances of detecting radiogenic effects, and provide an opportunity for lifetime studies of cancer incidence.

By contract with the International Agency for Research on Cancer (IARC), DCE is cooperating in an international radiation study to evaluate the risk of radiation exposure in cervical cancer in Europe. More than 22,000 patients treated for cervical cancer in 22 European clinics are being evaluated for the occurrence of second cancers subsequent to radiotherapy. Efforts are being made to quantify the risk of high- and low-level radiation doses and to evaluate the influence of host factors, such as age, on subsequent radiogenic risk. Fifteen cancer registries have been conducting cohort analyses on the risk of second cancers among 200,000 former cervical cancer patients. The cancer registry cohort analyses are almost complete and the findings are to be published as a monograph. The findings indicate excess risks, related to radiation, of cancers of the rectum, kidney, ovary, and corpus uteri, as well as acute nonlymphocytic leukemia. A deficit of breast cancer, possibly related to ovarian ablation, was also observed.

Among the notable activities in the environmental carcinogenesis program are the IARC monographs on the Evaluation of the Carcinogenic Risk of Chemicals to Humans, which are partially supported by a cooperative agreement with DCE. Thus far, 31 volumes have been published and several are in production; the volumes contain monographs in which the carcinogenic risk to man of chemicals, groups of chemicals and, more recently, of industrial and occupational exposures, is evaluated on the basis of results in experimental animals, studies in in vitro systems, and epidemiology. The monographs also contain background information on the chemicals under consideration such as chemical and physical properties, analysis occurrence, production, use and estimated human exposures from all sources. This information is provided to IARC by NCI through a resource contract held by SRI International. The IARC monographs have become a highly respected and authoritative reference source for countries around the world.

Another IARC activity supported under this agreement is the compilation of a listing of laboratories around the world into a compendium entitled "Survey of Chemicals Being Tested for Carcinogenicity." The IARC initiated this survey in 1973 on a worldwide basis; thus far ten surveys have been published and the eleventh survey is in preparation. These surveys are made available so that laboratories involved in carcinogenesis research, thus avoiding unnecessary duplication and serve as a useful current reference source for those engaged in bioassay work. The objectives of this project are two-fold. The first objective is to collect and evaluate existing carcinogenicity data on individual chemicals, groups of chemicals and industrial or occupational exposures. These evaluations are published in the monograph series described above. The second aim is to coordinate international efforts in carcinogenesis testing by identifying gaps in knowledge uncovered in the preparation of the monographs.

Personnel of DCE are actively involved in the NCI efforts under bilateral agreements with China (Mainland), France, Federal Republic of Germany, Italy, Japan, and the Soviet Union.

Division of Cancer Prevention and Control

The Division of Cancer Prevention and Control has awarded nine research grants to foreign institutions.

Scientists at the Ontario Institute for Studies in EDUC in Canada are studying the basic biology of clonogenic cells isolated from human bladder cancer. One of the research groups at the Montreal General Hospital Research Institute in Canada is studying a urinary polypeptide, putatively containing a colorectal organ-specific neoantigen. The antigen will be valuable in developing immunochemical procedures for determining circulating antibodies and for the clinical evaluation in the immunodiagnosis of colorectal cancer. Another research group at the same institution is studying a model system for the study of chronic pancreatic ductal obstruction and its relationship to pancreatic cancer. Scientists at the University of Waterloo, Canada, are doing preliminary studies on the effect of nicotine-bearing chewing gum in aiding in the cessation of smoking.

The Cancer Institute of the Chinese Academy of Medical Sciences in Beijing, China (Mainland), has received a grant to conduct two intervention trials using multiple vitamin-mineral supplements to evaluate the relation between such supplements and esophageal cancer mortality.

A research group at the Welsh National School of Medicine in Wales, United Kingdom, is studying a variety of histochemical methods for detecting and localizing steroid hormone receptors as well as protein hormones in human prostate tumor tissue, correlating the findings with the clinical response of patients to endocrine therapy.

The Center for Registration of Cancer and Allied Diseases in Jerusalem, Israel, is analyzing the incidence of cancer in Israel by geographic districts and the demographic and social characteristics of the population. The trend of cancer incidence of demographic groups will be compared with the trends in the United States.

The US-Finland Studies of Nutrition and Cancer has been started at the National Public Health Institute in Helsinki, Finland, on a collaborative chemoprevention trial of beta-carotene and vitamin E for lung cancer prevention among smoking men in Finland. Also, two case-control studies of nutritional factors in breast and other cancers will take place.

The Muhimbili Medical Center in Tanzania is conducting a study of chemoprevention of skin cancer using retinoids in a population of albino Africans.

In addition five individual research fellowships have been awarded to American scientists to study in foreign laboratories. Two of the NCI Fellows are studying in France, another two Fellows are studying in Israel, and one at the State University Hospital in Denmark.

Division of Cancer Treatment

The Division of Cancer Treatment has awarded research contracts to investigators in eight institutions of five foreign countries for studies related to the characterization of anticancer agents. These projects include:

BRISTOL LABORATORIES, INC.

This fermentation contract is designed primarily to obtain novel antitumor agents. This contract includes: 1) the preparation of fermentation beers from various unique microbes isolated in Bristol's Japanese facility, Bristol Banyu; 2) the use of ten different in vitro prescreens to evaluate the fermentations; 3) development of an in vitro assay to assist in quickly isolating the active anticancer agents; 4) dereplication of the materials to determine novelty; 5) chemical isolation of the active component; and 6) production of large quantities of new agents to thoroughly evaluate them in DCT screens.

INSTITUT JULES BORDET

Materials collected in Northern Europe are screened in vivo against animal tumors in accordance with established NCI protocols. Materials that originated in the U.S. or other countries may be sent to this laboratory for testing. Testing is currently being conducted at a level of approximately 11,000 L1210 test equivalents per year.

INSTITUTE OF CANCER RESEARCH

The objectives of this cost-sharing contract are to: 1) study the biochemical and pharmacological bases for treatment failure or response; 2) acquire or synthesize potential anticancer agents designed to increase the therapeutic efficacy of known drugs; 3) evaluate new compounds synthesized by the contractor, or of interest to NCI, against human tumor xenografts and mouse tumors unique to the contractor; and 4) conduct toxicological studies to establish safe dosage levels and regimens for clinical evaluation of the drugs in the United Kingdom.

ISTITUTO NAZIONALE PER LO STUDIO E LA CURA DEI TUMORI

A major effort in breast cancer has been undertaken through this contract. It has dealt primarily with adjuvant therapy of resectable disease, and its results have received worldwide attention. The institute has recently shown an improved overall survival for premenopausal patients treated with CMF. They also recently reported that 12 months of CMF is no more effective than six months. A reanalysis of disease-free survival among postmemopausal patients showed a clear advantage for patients receiving an average 75 percent drug dose compared to those 75 percent drug dose.

MICROBIAL CHEMISTRY RESEARCH FOUNDATION

The major objective of this contract is the isolation of new antitumor agents from fermentations of marine and terrestrial microorganisms. These fermentations are screened against various enzymatic and other biochemical screens. Active products are isolated in sufficient quantities to be evaluated at the National Cancer Institute. In addition, various immunogen tests have been developed to evaluate the organisms and their metabolites as potential immunological stimulators specific for cancers. One chemotherapeutic agent from this contract, aclacinomycin, is in Phase II clinical trials in the U.S. Toxicology has started on bactobolin and deoxyspergualin is being formulated. These compounds are in DN2B and DN2A, respectively.

JAPANESE FOUNDATION FOR CANCER RESEARCH

The objective of this contract is the maintenance of a chemotherapy liaison office at the Japanese Foundation for Cancer Research in Tokyo. The program is designed to foster close collaboration between Japanese and United States investigators in the development and application of new clinical anticancer drugs, and in the exchange of preclinical and clinical knowledge requisite for maximum progress in cancer therapy. A small testing facility is maintained for the screening and further evaluation of selected new compounds.

Through its "Cancer Chemotherapy Research Collaborative Office" at the Institut Jules Bordet in Brussels, Belgium, DCT maintains interaction with investigators of European nations concerning ongoing cancer research programs on both continents. The Brussels office has been especially useful in the areas of experimental and clinical pharmacology, clinical trials, and the organization of symposia jointly conducted by American and European investigators. It relates closely to the European pharmaceutical industry, providing a flow of new agents with potential anticancer activity. Fifty compounds are now in various stages of clinical development. The most recent initiative by the EORTC was to establish a New Drug Development Office with Professor H. Pinedo as director. This office was created to serve as the "executive arm" of the New Drug Development Committee to ensure that new drugs in development would move rapidly to the clinic. For example, it is the responsibility of this office to arrange for bulk synthesis, formulation, and toxicology; the office will work closely with the NCI Liaison Office in Brussels. This committee includes experts in biochemistry, pharmacology, toxicology, and medical oncology with NCI representation.

The Pan American Health Organization conducts collaborative treatment research with the best U.S. and Latin American investigators. The group's new administrative format, which focuses on the best collaborating institutions is working well. Recently, two Phase II studies of gastric cancer have been completed and two additional Phase II trials (isophosphamide, 4'epiadriamycin) are planned in this disease. In addition, an important randomized trial compared relative activity and toxicity of two platinum analogs (CBDCA and CHIPS) is planned for patients with previously untreated cervical carcinoma.

Personnel of DCT play key roles in the NCI bilateral agreements with China, Egypt, France, Federal Republic of Germany, Italy, Japan, and the Soviet Union through participation in: clinical trials; the evaluation of activity of substances indicating properties for biologic response modification; and programs in experimental/development therapeutics.

ANDRULIS RESEARCH CORPORATION (NO1-CO-44028)

Title: Current Cancer Research Project Analysis Center (CCRESPAC)

Contractor's Project Director: Mr. Robert Bruton (Acting)

Project Officer (NCI): Ms. Barbara Jaffe

Objectives: This contract includes two activities:

1) Preparing outlines of investigational cancer treatment protocols and using these summaries to update the CLINPROT and PDQ databases. (This activity was carried out by Informatics under contract NO1-CO-05509 until May 1984 at which time the subject contract was awarded to Andrulis, with Informatics continuing to provide the CLINPROT/PDQ activities as a subcontractor to Andrulis.)

2) The collection and processing of descriptions of ongoing research projects and using these project summaries to update the CANCERPROJ database.

Major Accomplishments: Activities required for monthly updating of the CLINPROT and PDQ databases have been carried out in a timely and highly accurate fashion. Plans to rebuild the CANCERPROJ database with current and accurate data have been formulated and the initial steps required for implementation of these plans have been successfully undertaken.

Proposed Course: Plans call for continuation of this two-year contract.

Date Contract Intitiated: May 5, 1984

Current Annual Level: $ 1,535,756

DEPARTMENT OF COMMERCE (National Technical Information Service) (Y01-CO-60702)

Title: SIB Document Announcement and Dissemination Services

Contractor's Project Director: Mr. James Jennings

Project Officer (NCI): Dr. John Schneider

Objective: This agreement supports the printing and dissemination of ICRDB/SIB publications, the announcements of these documents to potential users, and maintenance of all ICRDB/SIB documents in archival storage for supplying copies on request.

Major Accomplishments: Currently, NTIS disseminates more than 24,000 copies of CANCERGRAMs per month to over 12,000 investigators. In addition, more than five ONCOLOGY OVERVIEWS are published yearly, each of which is distributed to an average of 600 investigators. This contract also enables NTIS to act as collecting agency for charges incurred by use of access codes when users search the cancer databases on the NLM system.

Significance to Biomedical Research and Program of the Institute: This interagency agreement has allowed the SIB to rapidly fulfill one of its mandated activities, namely, the broad dissemination of biomedical research information on cancer. Through its various worldwide outlets, NTIS performs a valuable service in disseminating SIB products to the global scientific community.

Proposed Course: The agreement will continue as described.

Date Agreement Initiated: September 30, 1976

Current Annual Level: $634,194

FRANKLIN RESEARCH INSTITUTE (NO1-CO-14343)

Title: Cancer Information Dissemination and Analysis Center (CIDAC) for Carcinogenesis

Contractor's Project Director: Dr. Richard Mason

Project Officer: Dr. Dianne E. Tingley

Objectives: The CIDAC provides scientific input necessary to produce information products and services for cancer researchers, and provides guidance to the ICRDB Section, in the area of carcinogenesis.

Major Accomplishments: The CIDAD regularly produces 21 monthly CANCERGRAMs, current awareness bulletins containing abstracts of recently published literature, and an annual compilation of abstracts of carcinogenesis-related review articles as a supplement to the CANCERGRAMs, under the title "Recent Reviews in Carcinogenesis." ONCOLOGY OVERVIEWS, retrospective bibliographies with abstracts concerning high interest topics in carcinogenesis research, are published annually. The CIDAC also performs custom searches of the CANCERLINE databases in response to requests for information; submits monthly Highlight Reports, pinpointing significant new developments in carcinogenesis research; and assists in database quality control.

Significance to Biomedical Research and Program of the Institute: The CIDAC serves as a valuable resource for the NCI and the worldwide cancer research community in the area of carcinogenesis. The CANCERGRAMs collectively provide comprehensive coverage of this entire field, quickly alerting researchers to new findings with minimal expenditure of effort, thereby allowing them more time for productive research. ONCOLOGY OVERVIEWS enable researchers to rapidly update their knowledge in emerging areas of research concentration.

Proposed Course: This contract terminated in May 1984. The activity will be continued through a new contract awarded as a result of current recompetition.

Date Contract Initiated: May 4, 1978

Current Annual Level: $315,597

FRANKLIN RESEARCH INSTITUTE (N01-CO-14356)

Title: Cancer Information Dissemination and Analysis Center (CIDAC) for Cancer Virology, Immunology, and Basic Cancer Biology (VIB)

Contractor's Project Director: Dr. Gerald Soslau

Project Officer: Dr. Dianne E. Tingley

Objectives: The CIDAC provides scientific input necessary to produce information products and services for cancer researchers, and provides guidance to the ICRDB Section, in the area of cancer virology, immunology, and basic cancer biology.

Major Accomplishments: The CIDAC regularly produces 24 monthly CANCERGRAMs, current awareness bulletins containing abstracts of recently published literature. Five ONCOLOGY OVERVIEWS, retrospective bibliographies with abstracts concerning high interest topics in basic cancer research, are published annually. The CIDAC also performs custom searches of the CANCERLINE databases in response to requests for information; submits monthly Highlight Reports, pinpointing significant new developments in basic cancer research; and assists in database quality control.

Significance to Biomedical Research and Program of the Institute: The CIDAC serves as a valuable resource for the NCI and the worldwide cancer research community in the area of cancer virology, immunology, and biology. The CANCERGRAMs collectively provide comprehensive coverage of this entire field, quickly alerting researchers to new findings with minimal expenditure of effort and thereby allowing them more time for productive research. ONCOLOGY OVERVIEWS enable researchers to rapidly update their knowledge in emerging areas of research concentration.

Proposed Course: The contractor will continue production of CANCERGRAMs and ONCOLOGY OVERVIEWS and provision of information services.

Date Contract Initiated: June 22, 1976

Current Annual Level: $318,432

IIT RESEARCH INSTITUTE (N01-CO-05468)

Title: Computer Support for Cancer Information Dissemination

Contractor's Project Director: Susan Goyer

Project Officer (NCI): Dr. Ihor J. Masnyk

Objectives: The purpose of the contract is to establish and operate a Computer Support Center (CSC) for the ICRDB Section.

Major Accomplishments: The contractor performs a wide variety of computer operations necessary for the creation and maintenance of ICRDB databases, preparation of ICRDB publications, maintenance of special mailing lists, the PDQ Knowledge Base/Information System, statistical reporting and special tasks identified by the Section.

Significance to Biomedical Research and Program of the Institute: The computer support provided by the contractor is of central importance to the entire spectrum of ICRDB products and services, whereby the Section is able to fulfill its mandate to actively promote the dissemination of cancer research information on a worldwide basis.

Proposed Course: Plans call for continuation of this contract through February 26 1985.

Date Contract Initiated: June 27, 1975

Current Annual Level: $649,883

INFORMATICS, INC. (NO1-CO-14361)

Title: Technical Support Services for the International Cancer Research Data Bank (ICRDB) and the Office of International Affairs (OIA)

Contractor's Project Director: Mr. Richard Amacher

Project Officer: Dr. J. Wesley Simmons

Objectives: This project provides a broad range of technical support activity to cancer-related information activities within the OIA.

Major Accomplishments: Significant effort was provided for the support of PDQ in the form of updating the Directory File and in the areas of promotion and marketing of this database. Support relating to exhibits at major cancer meetings has contributed significantly to the enhancement of user awareness of ICRDB products and services. Ongoing updates of publication mailing lists preclude unnecessary mailing of ICRDB publications.

Significance to Biomedical Research and Programs of the Institute: This project makes available, as needed, personnel, expertise, and equipment for support in the areas of publications preparation, promotion of user awareness, evaluation of user services, and scientific analysis. This support is essential to the fulfillment of the ICRDB mandate for active collection and dissemination of cancer research information.

Proposed Course: The present contract will continue, with special efforts devoted to support of PDQ and other OIA activities.

Date Contract Initiated: August 31, 1981

Current Annual Level: $301,486

INFORMATION VENTURES, INC. (NO1-CO-44026)

Title: Screening, Indexing, Abstracting, and Keying of Cancer-related Literature

Contractor's Project Director: Dr. Bruce Kleinstein

Project Officer (NCI): Mr. James Carter

Objectives: The SIAK project collects, indexes, and keys abstracts presented at meetings which describe cancer research projects. The project also indexes and keys abstracts of books and other documents not covered by NLM. These abstracts are part of the source material for CANCERLIT, CANCERGRAMs, and ONCOLOGY OVERVIEWS.

Major Accomplishments: Approximately 1,000 items are processed each month and forwarded to the ICRDB computer contractor for the final reformatting required to update the computer database. The abstracts are collected from major biomedical conferences such as the American Association for Cancer Research, the American Society of Clinical Oncology, and the Federation of American Societies for Experimental Biology.

Significance to Biomedical Research and Program of the Institute: The SIAK project provides rapid, easy access to cancer research information presented at meetings and other sources not covered by NLM. This information can be retrieved by searching the CANCERLIT databases in any narrow topical area of cancer.

Proposed Course: The project will continue with no anticipated change for a four-year period.

Date Contract Initiated: February 22, 1984

Current Annual Level: $324,081

INTERNATIONAL AGENCY FOR RESEARCH ON CANCER (N01-CO-55195)

Title: Clearinghouse for Ongoing Work in Cancer Epidemiology

Contractor's Project Director: Dr. Calum S. Muir

Project Officer (NCI): Dr. J. Wesley Simmons

Objectives: This contract provides a special mechanism for intensive collection and dissemination of information about current cancer-related epidemiology projects.

Major Accomplishments: The Clearinghouse, located in Lyon, France, continuously identifies and contacts new sources of epidemiology research project descriptions. Project descriptions are collected, edited, and published annually as the Directory of On-going Research in Cancer Epidemiology. This information is also provided on magnetic tape for entry into the CANCERPROJ database. Approximately 1,300 ongoing projects are listed in this Directory.

Significance to Biomedical Research and Program of the Institute: By serving as a resource for epidemiological data and establishing communication among epidemiology researchers worldwide, the Clearinghouse promotes international awareness and cooperation which contributes to more productive research in this area.

Proposed Course: Work will continue as described.

Date Contract Initiated: February 25, 1975

Current Annual Level: $136,907

METROTEC, INC. (263-82-C-0260)

Title: Editorial Support Services

Contractor's Project Director: Mr. Jack Nelson

Project Officer (NCI): Anne McCarthy

Objectives: This agreement with Metrotec, Inc., provides for the editorial services necessary to publish Cancer Treatment Symposia, a resource of the NCI that facilitates the timely and effective transfer of newly developed technology to physicians in the community so that the current results of therapeutic research can be more widely applied.

Major Accomplishments: Metrotec, Inc., has provided editorial services for the publication of four symposia:

- Proceedings of the US-Japan Meeting on Drug Development and Cancer Treatment Research. Cancer Treat Symp 1:1-117, 1983.
- Proceedings of the Workshop on Patterns of Failure After Cancer Treatment. Cancer Treat Symp 2:1-313, 1983.
- The Interdisciplinary Program for Radiation Oncology Research. Cancer Treat Symp 1:1-191, 1984.
- Proceedings of the Workshop on 2'-Deoxycoformycin: Current Status and Future Directions. Cancer Treat Symp 2:1-109, 1984.

Significance to Biomedical Research and Program of the Institute: The need for publishing a symposium arises when a particular area of clinical research reaches a critical stage. It is then that a conference is held to summarize available data, to determine clinical applications, to generate new questions for investigation, and to determine priorities for future research. Prompt publication of the proceedings of these meetings is the best means of disseminating this scientific information and of facilitating the translation of research into clinical practice.

As cancer therapy has become more effective and widely applied by physicians in the community, there has been a corresponding increase in the need to synthesize data and define clinical applications of therapeutic research and to facilitate the rapid dissemination of information about the toxic effects of therapeutic agents. One of the most effective solutions to the problems of technology transfer is expeditious publication and distribution to the medical community. In addition, publication of the results of clinical trials opens the data to the scrutiny of other scientists who wish to repeat the therapeutic experiment.

Proposed Course: This 3-year contract expires in July 26, 1985.

Date Contract Initiated: July 27, 1982

Current Annual Value: $89,451

NATIONAL ACADEMY OF SCIENCES (NAS) (N01-CO-44027)

Title: Support of Activities of the USA National Committee for the International Union Against Cancer (UICC)

Contractor's Project Director: June Ewing

Project Officer (NCI): Barry M. Goldfarb

Objectives: This contract serves the dual purpose of: 1) providing for one representative body (acting on behalf of the various U.S. cancer organizations and foundations) to deal with issues and policies on the International Union Against Cancer (UICC); and 2) supporting Committee participation in the UICC-sponsored International Cancer Congress held every four years.

Major Accomplishments: Planning for the XIV International Cancer Congress to be held in Budapest, Hungary, in September 1986.

Significance to Biomedical Research and Program of the Institute: This contract supports the representative body which develops and presents the issues and policies of the United States cancer research community to the UICC, and through support of the International Cancer Congresses, promotes the productive exchange of research information among researchers throughout the world.

Proposed Course: Plans call for continuation of this contract through January 15, 1988.

Date Contract Initiated: January 16, 1984

Current Annual Level: $35,000

NATIONAL LIBRARY OF MEDICINE (Y02-CO-30708)

Title: Joint NLM/NCI Interagency Agreement

Contractor's Project Director: Mr. John Anderson

Project Officer (NCI): Dr. Dianne E. Tingley

Objectives: This agreement with the NLM provides for the generation, maintenance, and operation of the NCI databases and systems (PDQ, CANCERLIT, CANCEREXPRESS, CANCERPROJ, CLINPROT) on the NLM computer, and for dissemination of information in these collections to institutions subscribing to the NLM computer services.

Major Accomplishments: The NLM contributes cancer abstracts prepared for the MEDLARS system as a major component of the input for cancer literature databases. The NLM also maintains and updates NCI's online cancer databases containing approximately 400,000 abstracts of published literature, 10,000 high quality abstracts from the most recent four-month period, 20,000 descriptions of research projects, and 4,500 summaries of clinical protocols for the ICRDB Section. In addition, the NLM maintains and updates PDQ with state-of-the-art information on diagnosis, prognosis, staging, and treatment information about 82 different types of cancer, as well as the names, addresses, and telephone numbers of physicians and organizations specializing in the treatment of cancer. Databases are updated/regenerated on a monthly basis. It is estimated that over 40,000 searches were run against cancer databases in FY 1983.

Significance to Biomedical Research and Program of the Institute: In consonance with the National Cancer Act of 1971, this interagency agreement has given the NCI the cost savings benefit of using an existing organization with capabilities to reformat, process, and make the results of cancer research available to more than 2,500 locations throughout the world via an existing telecommunications network resident at NLM. These locations include medical schools, medical research institutions, regional medical libraries, and hospitals throughout the United States and several countries outside the United States.

Proposed Course: This agreement will continue indefinitely.

Date Contract Initiated: May 1, 1983

Current Annual Level: $710,000

PAN AMERICAN HEALTH ORGANIZATION (N01-CO-65332)

Title: Latin American Cancer Research Information Program (LACRIP)

Contractor's Project Director: Dr. Jorge Litvak

Project Officer (NCI): Dr. J. Wesley Simmons

Major Accomplishments: The contractor has supplied several hundred cancer-related articles and meeting abstracts from Latin America for inclusion in CANCERLIT. There is a steady input of summaries of cancer research projects and clinical protocols for inclusion into the NCI databases, CANCERPROJ, CLINPROT, and eventually PDQ.

Significance to Biomedical Research and Program of the Institute: LACRIP is an important resource for the Office of International Affairs in that it supplies project descriptions, clinical protocols, and journal articles for the databases (CANCERPROJ, CLINPROT, and eventually PDQ) that would otherwise not be included, and provides a centralized mechanism for dissemination of cancer-related information to a large number of countries in Latin America.

Proposed Course: A new contract was awarded July 31, 1984, for a period of three years.

Date Contract Initiated: May 24, 1976

Current Annual Level: $226,696

PROMIS INFORMATION SYSTEMS (N01-CO-33877)

Title: Development, Implementation, and Operation of an NCI Information System for PDQ2.

Contractor's Project Director: Dr. Peter L. Walton

Project Officer (NCI): Dr. Robert J. Esterday, Jr.

Objectives: The Physician Data Query (PDQ) Information System is being developed by the NCI to be a fully integrated, computerized knowledge base providing rapid retrieval of state-of-the-art cancer treatment information.

Major Accomplishments: NCI has developed a nationwide computerized information database called PDQ. PDQ is a geographically matrixed, centralized information source designed to assist physicians by listing treatment options and research protocols for specific cancers, and a directory of physicians and organizations/institutions who have the interest and experience in the management of cancer patients. NCI altered one of its major information databases (CLINPROT) to provide primary care physicians with detailed information on cancer treatment options. This database, now known as PDQ1 was made available in October 1982 through the National Library of Medicine (NLM), MEDLARS System at many hospitals, medical libraries, universities, and medical schools.

The PDQ1 database gives the names and institution contacts for physicians at NCI-funded institutions that belong to clinical trial groups and cancer centers throughout the United States. PDQ1 contains approximately 1,000 active treatment protocols. The database is updated monthly and operates under ELHILL files and retrieval software (MEDLARS II) at NLM.

Under this contract NCI is developing an expanded database known as PDQ2. This knowledge base/information system has multiple, tightly integrated (linked) files or sets of information. The files are described in the CCB Section of the annual report for FY 1984.

NCI is producing PDQ2 as an external tape output of the integrated files for distribution by NLM, utilizing the INQUIRE Data Base Management System (DBMS) software, and by other private information vendors that have an easy-to-use, interactive DBMS software. For example, PDQ/INQUIRE makes searches easy, even for someone relatively inexperienced with computers. With a "user-friendly" system, the user unknowingly searches multiple, linked files as if they were a single file.

Under this contract, NCI obtained a perpetual use license for the proprietary ATLAS software system. ATLAS is unique, in that its files are not fixed length, applications programming written outside the DBMS is not required, a separate query language (a different set of software) which is not integrated with the DBMS is not necessary. Separate report generation software is not required since ATLAS is completely integrated and further, other systems require separate programs for editing, text processing, and data processing. This is not required by ATLAS. ATLAS is the core of the PDQ production system. It is a network DBMS which can be best described as a "program-less" system. Programming code does not have to be written to modify the PDQ production system application. Under this contract, NCI has now installed an operating network of Sperry-Univac minicomputers with high-speed, touch-screen terminals that operate over a broad-band local area network at the R.A. Bloch International Cancer Information Center.

Significance to Biomedical Research and Program of the Institute: Upon implementation of the PDQ2 system, the effective treatment of cancer can be enhanced by dissemination of state-of-the-art information. It is expected this will reduce the mortality for all forms of cancer. Since there are numerous research efforts throughout the United States, successful new treatment methods may not reach all who might benefit.

PDQ2 will shorten the time lag by informing physicians and their cancer patients of organizations/institutions using the latest available protocols. It is the opinion of the Director, NCI, that an estimated 3,000 - 4,000 lives can be saved in a year if this system is implemented nationally.

Proposed Course: This contract will be completed on September 21, 1984.

Date Contract Initiated: March 22, 1983

Current Annual Level: $780,445

UNION INTERNATIONALE CONTRE LE CANCER (UICC) (NO1-CO-65341)

Title: International Scientist-to-Scientist Information Exchange Program

Contractor's Project Director: Dr. Anders Englund

Project Officer (NCI): Dr. Robert R. Omata and Dr. J. Wesley Simmons

Objectives: The purpose of this program is to promote direct and rapid person-to-person transfer of information about new or improved technology or methodology between investigators from different countries who are working in areas of basic, clinical or behavioral research, in order to further the progress of cancer research.

Major Accomplishments: This contract promotes international cancer research collaboration by providing International Cancer Research Technology Transfer (ICRETT) awards which enable two cancer researchers from different countries to jointly carry out brief research projects. From the inception of this program through March 1984, 713 exchanges (average period sponsored is three weeks) have been granted.

Significance to Biomedical Research and Program of the Institute: Scientists are afforded the valuable opportunity for on-the-spot collaboration necessary for comparing the results of parallel or related reserach and developing or improving techniques. These interactions frequently lead to continuing exchange of research information, which in turn leads to a more productive collaborative effort.

Proposed Course: This contract activity will continue at approximately the same level through March 1989.

Date Contract Initiated: December 4, 1975

Current Annual Level: $100,000

UNION INTERNATIONAL CONTRE LE CANCER (UICC) (NO1-CO-75377)

Title: Liaison and Implementation Projects in Support of the NCI, International Cancer Research Data Bank (ICRDB) Section

Contractor's Project Director: Dr. Gerald P. Warwick

Project Officer (NCI): Barry M. Goldfarb

Objectives: Through its Committee on International Collaborative Activities (CICA), the UICC provides liaison and implementation projects in support of the International Cancer Research Data Bank (ICRDB) Section.

Major Accomplishments: This effort has resulted in collection and processing of information on over 6,500 unpublished current cancer research projects. This information is made available worldwide through the CANCERPROJ database. This project has also resulted in the development, as a pilot program, of an International Cancer Patient Data Exchange System (ICPDES) whereby information covering the entire patient care spectrum is collected in an internationally standardized manner, with participation by 5 major U.S. and 11 foreign cancer centers. As of November 1983, over 45,500 case reports had been entered.

Significance to Biomedical Research and Program of the Institute: CICA activities have been of major significance in making the ICRDB Section truly international in scope. Active efforts to establish liaison with and obtain data from cancer centers and individual investigators around the world have simulated increased communication and cooperation among researchers, as well as more effective utilization of clinical and basic research data.

Proposed Course: Patient data collection will continue through the ICPDES, and a European data processing center in Amsterdam has been established in addition to one located in Houston. Plans for a new edition of the International Directory of Specialized Cancer Research and Treatment Establishments, last published in 1982, listing 679 such centers located in 80 countries, are being prepared.

Date Contract Initiated: April 1, 1977

Current Annual Level: $225,000

UNIVERSITY OF TEXAS SYSTEM CANCER CENTER (N01-CO-14347)

Title: Cancer Information Dissemination and Analysis Center (CIDAC) for Cancer Diagnosis and Therapy

Contractor's Project Director: Dr. Eugene McKelvey

Project Officer (NCI): Dr. Dianne E. Tingley

Objectives: The CIDAC provides scientific input necessary to produce information products and services for cancer researchers, and provides guidance to the ICRDB Section, in the area of cancer diagnosis, therapy, and rehabilitation.

Major Accomplishments: The CIDAC regularly produces 21 monthly CANCERGRAMs, current awareness bulletins containing abstracts of recently published literature. Five ONCOLOGY OVERVIEWS, retrospective bibliographies with abstracts concerning high interest topics in clinical cancer research, are published annualled. This CIDAC performs custom searches of the CANCERLINE databases in response to requests for information; submits monthly Highlight Reports, pinpointing significant new developments in clinical cancer research; and assists in database quality control. This CIDAC also provides input used for updating PDQ.

Significance to Biomedical Research and Program of the Institute: The CIDAC serves as a valuable resource for the NCI and the worldwide cancer research community in the area of oncology research. The CANCERGRAMs collectively provide comprehensive coverage of this entire field, quickly alerting researchers to new findings with minimal expenditure of effort, thereby allowing them more time for productive research. ONCOLOGY OVERVIEWS enable researchers to rapidly update their knowledge in emerging areas of research concentration.

Proposed Course: The contractor will continue production of CANCERGRAMs and ONCOLOGY OVERVIEWS and provision of information services.

Date Contract Initiated: June 24, 1976

Current Annual Level: $352,679

Equal Employment Opportunity Office (EEO)
Office of the Director
National Cancer Institute

Summary Report

October 1, 1983 through September 30, 1984

The second FEORP/Affirmative Action Plan (AAP) assessment report was prepared and distributed during the month of May 1984. The plan will be monitored on an annual basis instead of semi-annual as anticipated. The Invitation to Careers in Research (ICR) program, an NCI pilot project to provide minority students at elementary and secondary levels with an opportunity to learn about the biomedical research program and to encourage excellence in the study of science, will implement its second phase in the fall in several District of Columbia schools.

The Federal Equal Opportunity Recruitment Program (FEORP) Plan for Disabled Individuals and Disabled Veterans for FY 1984-1986 was developed and has been approved by the NIH. The handicapped individuals and disabled veterans network was expanded to include several local organizations, school programs, and local veterans administration offices.

Lunch time seminars were presented throughout the year; Office Automation, Stress Management and films during Women's History Week of 1984.

Recruitment activities were conducted at several minority universities and a recruitment network was established with the Indians into Medicine (INMED) Program of the School of Medicine at the University of North Dakota, this project resulted in the hiring of three Native Americans into laboratory support positions in DCE (2 as summer students, one on a temporary appointment) and a continuing communications system between NCI and the INMED Program.

OFFICE OF ADMINISTRATIVE MANAGEMENT
OFFICE OF THE DIRECTOR
NATIONAL CANCER INSTITUTE

Program Activities Report
October 1, 1983 - September 30, 1984

The Office of Administrative Management (OAM) coordinates and manages all administrative activities of the Institute and is headed by the Associate Director for Administrative Management who also serves as Executive Officer. The Office is composed of seven branches; Management Analysis Branch, Administrative Services Branch, Personnel Management Branch, Research Contracts Branch, Grants Administration Branch, Extramural Financial Data Branch, and Financial Management Branch.

Some notable activities of the OAM during Fiscal Year 1984 include:

- PDQ: PDQ is now operational and is serving as a resource for physicians to aid in the treatment and referral of cancer patients.

- Contract Management: The DHHS Office of Procurement Assistance and Logistics completed their final review which confirmed the effective implementation of planned improvements in contract management.

The achievements of the individual branches of the Office are described below:

Administrative Services Branch (ASB)

The ASB serves as the Administrative Office for all of the components of the Office of the Director, including the Office of Administrative Management, Office of Cancer Communications, Office of International Affairs, and the Office of Program Planning and Analysis. It is responsible for office services, property management, mail and files, international travel, domestic travel policy (including the annual travel plan for the Institute), and space management. ASB serves as the NCI coordinating point for cross-cutting administrative issues.

- Travel and Property Control: Comprehensive courses on travel and property inventory and control were developed and presented by the ASB Travel and Property Unit. These courses were developed to complement the NIH courses on these same subjects and to instruct NCI travel and property control personnel in local procedures that are unique to the NCI.

- Procurement: Small purchase procurement procedures were revamped and streamlined in the areas of review and clearance. This new system provides much quicker turn-around and enhances the ability to run status checks which has resulted in a 20% improvement in procurement processing time.

Financial Management Branch (FMB)

The FMB serves as principal advisor to the Institute in the financial management aspects of the planning, formulation, execution and evaluation of its programs. It collaborates with the Office of Program Planning and Analysis in the development and coordination of the National Cancer Plan with the budget plans and monitors the execution of the Institute's financial management program.

- Office Computerization: The Branch has further computerized its functions through the acquisition of a personal computer with graphics capabilities. On-site training was conducted for all professional staff in the use of applicable software. Projects now possible through the use of new computer capabilities include daily status of funds report, tracking of FTE usage, communications with mainframe computers and numerous other reports.

- Other Computer Developments: Using the NIH 7000 and CT 45, reduced the volume of data contained in both the operating budget and status of funds reports sent to Divisions. This was accomplished by reorganizing data presentation and by partial redesign of the operating budget system. Reduced distribution time of these reports from three days to one.

Research Contracts Branch (RCB)

RCB participates in developing policies on Institute research contract programs; develops guidelines, procedures and controls to promote compliance with policy and sound contracting practices; provides contract management services for all Institute research contracts; and implements automated Institute contract management information systems.

- Improvements Implemented: Final review by the DHHS Office of Procurement Assistance and Logistics initiated in 1981 confirmed that the Branch has effectively implemented improvements in its contracting process.

- FCRF Support: The proposed acquisition of a supercomputer for FCRF required significant support by the RCB in the planning of a procurement strategy and in the resolution of substantial policy questions to implement this extremely important acquisition.

- Pre-Award Tracking System (PATS): The Pre-Award Tracking System was fully implemented. The reports generated by this automated system which tracks approximately 20 steps in the pre-award cycle has proved to be an effective management tool in facilitating the timely award of NCI contracts.

- FCRF Reorganization: The FCRF contracting operation has been officially designated as a Section in this Branch. This is in recognition of the substantial role this office has in the operation of a complex research facility.

- The Federal Acquisition Regulations: Conversion to the Federal Acquisition Regulations (FAR) which replace the Federal Procurement Regulations has been fully implemented. The FAR is a uniform codification of all the regulations applicable to contracting. RCB developed the standard Request For Proposal and contract format for the NIH.

- An Automated Computer-based System for Preparation of Requests for Proposal (RFP): An automated RFP was examined by NCI for use at the NIH. As a result of NCI's efforts, the NIH will be the lead agency in a DHHS sponsored effort to implement the system Department-wide.

- Pay Back System for Researchers: The Frederick Contract Section provides substantial support in implementing a pay back system for research services which are now available to NIH intramural researchers.

Extramural Financial Data Branch (EFDB)

EFDB is responsible for maintaining grants financial data, performing the analyses necessary to provide funding guideline recommendations, preparing of budgets and advice on grants financial policy decisions, and for making grants financial data available to requestors. In addition, EFDB monitors the Contracts Management System (CMS), Pre-Award Tracking System (PATS), and Contracts Administration Systems (CAS) in order to provide information system services for program, review, and contracting staff.

- The Funding Plan Procedures Manual: The Funding Plan Procedures Manual was printed and distributed in 1984. The manual is intended to provide NCI staff with an understanding of the NCI grant funding process and procedures.

- The Financial Data Book: The Financial Data Book was reformatted to eliminate duplications, improve organization, and add contract data. A system was developed so that most of the tables in the book could be produced by computer program.

- Contracts Management System: EFDB, and the Research Contracts Branch (RCB) evaluated the Contract Management System (CMS), Pre-Award Tracking System (PATS), and Contract Administration System (CAS) to determine steps necessary to upgrade and eventually integrate the three systems. In the meantime, several improvements have been made to the CMS to enhance data integrity; add relevant data fields; and convert to a far more efficient programming language.

- CMS Improvements: A plan was developed for the direct interaction of users with CMS for data input and receipt of reports.

- PATS System: During 1984 the PATS became fully operational and PATS on-line reports became available. These enable users to view full-screen copies of selected reports on their telecommunications terminals.

- CAS Redesign: EFDB coordinated efforts to redesign the CAS. Conversion of CAS to a more efficient programming language (SAS) will enable users to generate reports and new data on-line. The new system eliminates many duplications in the old system while providing more efficient and accurate listings.

- Financial Data System: The development of the Financial Data System continued with the merging of information from the EFDB 1984 data files and the IMPAG grants data files at the end of fiscal year 1984. The system is being developed to provide an easily accessible data processing resource from which users can produce a series of adaptable reports. The database has been designed to be flexible enough to provide for possible merging with other systems such as the DFM Central Accounting System.

Grants Administration Branch (GAB)

The GAB performs all business activities attendant to the administration of NCI grant and cooperative agreement programs. It participates with the Division Directors and their staffs in the formulation and execution of grant policy, develops the Institute's position on grant and cooperative agreement management issues, and negotiates the amount of awards. During FY 1984, NCI issued approximately 6,000 award notices for 4,000 grants and cooperative agreements totaling $674 million.

- Equalization of Workload: In order to move awards out of the heaviest workload period, the fourth quarter of the fiscal year, a plan has been devised and approved to cycle awards into other quarters over the course of the next 3 to 4 fiscal years.

- Small Business Innovative Research (SBIR): Phase I of this new program started at the end of FY 83. In FY 84, Phase II will go into effect. Approximately 16 Phase I applications have been approved and will go to the NCAB for possible award this summer. Approximately 48 Phase I, and 15 Phase II SBIR grants have been received for NCAB review this fall with approved grants to be awarded this fiscal year.

- Acquired Immune Deficiency Syndrome (AIDS): Eleven new cooperative agreements in the Aids program have been funded. It is anticipated that a total of 29 awards for $5.5 million will be made this fiscal year.

- Organizational Changes: The Grants Policy, Operations Analysis and Audit Section was established under the Office of the Chief to help coordinate Branch administrative activities.

- Support Staff Implementations: We have established Grants Technical Assistant (GTA) positions to provide a career development opportunity for clerk-typists and secretaries.

- Issuances and Publications: The following NCI policy and GAB Guidelines were issued this year:

NCI	1.02	Administrative Increases for Salaries
GAB	3.06	Alterations and Renovations

GAB	3.15	Detailed Budget Recommendations Forms/Revised Budgets
GAB	3.17	Documentation of Grant Files
GAB	4.02	Change Notices/Revised Awards
NCI	5.05	Addendum to the Cooperative Agreement Policy

- GAB Retreat: As a result of the October 1983 GAB Retreat which highlighted areas in which changes might be made to strengthen GAB administration, many changes have already been put into effect and others are underway. For instance, a study of the pilot microfiche program was made, recommendations were presented to enhance the utility of the files by microfiching all historical files while maintaining current working files in paper form.

Personnel Management Branch (PMB): The PMB exercises appointing authority and provides central personnel management services for the entire NCI including policy development, training, workforce planning, recruitment, employee development, salary administration and equal employment opportunity in collaboration with the NCI EEO Coordinator.

- Special Activities: The Personnel Officer served as the key staff person for the NIH Subcommittee on Personnel Functions. The Subcommittee on Functions was part of the top-level steering committee chaired by the Deputy Director, NIH which was established to evaluate all aspects of the personnel management program at NIH. The work of the subcommittee focused essentially on the streamlining of personnel functions and redistribution of work activities to achieve agency mandated cuts in personnel staff, with minimum disruption of on-going personnel activities. The final report of the subcommittee will be transmitted as the NIH position on Reform 88 personnel/payroll initiative to the Assistant Secretary for Personnel Administration, DHHS.

- Recruitment Activities: The NCI Staffing Office participated in several special initiatives to meet the staffing needs of the various NCI Divisions. Some examples are:

  - the NCI Special Training Program initiated to give qualified applicants research training in the areas of epidemiology, molecular carcinogenesis, nutrition in cancer prevention and treatment and cancer control.

  - the Cancer Control Science Associates Program of the Division of Cancer Prevention and Control (DCPC) which is designed to increase the number of scientists who are interested in, oriented toward and qualified to conduct cancer control intervention research.

  - A mass recruitment campaign for laboratory support positions. Over 1500 schools were contacted and were provided information on recruitment of laboratory support candidates and the 1984 NCI Summer Program.

  - the 1984 Summer Program was successfully completed filling approximately 200 positions in clerical, undergraduate, and graduate programs.

- a special recruiting visit was made to the American Public Health Association Conference in Dallas, Texas to fill Branch Chief, Epidemiologist and Statistician positions in the Division of Cancer Prevention and Control.

The Staffing Office assumed special responsibility for providing highly qualified candidates for laboratory technical support positions to OPM, as well as meeting our internal needs. This was accomplished by:

1. Developing a recruitment calendar for the 1983-84 school year and conducting visits to 31 colleges and universities which resulted in the receipt of approximately 500 applications.

2. Placing advertisements in the Washington Post and in Science for laboratory technical support positions. Approximately 300 applications were received from this effort.

3. Placing an employer profile in the 1984 issue of Peterson's, a guide designed for those interested in research careers and employment in science engineering and computer fields. Fifteen thousand (15,000) copies of this issue were distributed.

Exhibit and Recruitment Materials: The Staffing Office updated the following exhibit and recruitment materials:

1. Developed a Clerk-Typist brochure to be used for recruitment trips to local high schools and business schools. This brochure highlights the opportunities and training available for participants in the program, qualifications requirements and salary and benefits information.

2. Developed a recruitment film about NCI, including the organization and mission, legislative history, and past, present and future developments in cancer research.

° Personnel Operations: The establishment of special pay rates for the GS-648, Therapeutic Radiologic Technologists was approved by OPM and became effective on October 2, 1983. This helped facilitate recruitment efforts for these much needed technicians.

A Team Supervisor served on a Billet Study Group for the pilot test of the proposed revised Billet Description and Evaluation Plan for the Commissioned Corps. This resulted in the recommendation to drastically revise the proposed plan.

° Computerization and Office Automation: Designed and implemented a computerized system to capture Merit Promotion recruitment data and FEORP statistics.

The automation of the Request for Personnel Action (SF-52) process is progressing. The Statement of Work has been written, a potential contractor identified and negotiations have been initiated.

- Information/Publications: Developed or presented the following information:

    1. Guidance on handling Staff Fellowship applications

    2. General instructions to be used when medical information ("fitness for duty") is required for an employee

    3. Procedures/instructions for use by deciding officials in adverse action cases

    4. Information for supervisors on establishing an SES position

    5. Procedures to be used for personnel actions involving physicians with patient care responsibilities.

    6. Publication of a new chapter in the Manager/Supervisor Handbook: "Taking Action on the Troubled Employee."

    7. A program for administrative staff on "How to Conduct Effective Interviews in the Selection of Employees."

  PMB Manual Issuances and Instruction and Information Memoranda

    Maintaining OPF's
    Processing Physician Comparability Allowance
    Processing Name Changes
    NCI Policy on Cancelled or Incomplete Training

- Training:

    1. NCI Employee Training Data System: Implemented the NCI Employee Training Data System. Reports generated from the NCI system can provide detailed analysis on NCI training trends, needs and expenditures.

    2. Arranged for on-site OPM courses on Interpersonal Communications for all PMB staff and on Travel Procedures for NCI staff.

Management Analysis Branch (MAB):

The MAB serves as a staff resource for the Institute providing advice and guidance on the administration and management of the NCI. Specific areas of activity include providing advice on the development, implementation and interpretation of policy and regulations; performance of management studies and surveys; analysis of organizational proposals and provision of advice on organizational structure and the preparation of special analyses and reports on the administrative aspects of Institute operations or programs.

- Staffing Analysis: Prepared an analysis of staffing at the branch and section levels within the Institute to improve the efficiency of manpower resource utilization.

- Filing Handbook: Prepared a Self-Help Filing Handbook to assist NCI staff with the organization and management of filed material.

- Comments: Coordinated comments on: the President's Private Sector Task Force Report on R&D; IG draft report on "Review of Purchases of Drugs and Medical Supplies by the Public Health Service" in order to communicate NCI's views on these matters.

- Microfiche Study: Performed an analysis of the feasibility of the use of microfilm/microfiche systems in the Personnel Management Branch.

- Quality Control Analysis: Performed a quality control analysis of a representative sample of Merit Pay plans.

- Vehicle Usage at FCRF: Performed a study of vehicle usage at the Frederick Cancer Research Facility in order to help insure the most efficient utilization of resources.

- Study of OD Central Files Operations: Performed a study and prepared recommendations on methods to improve operations and maximize efficient use of space in the NCI Central Files operation.

- Organizational Change: Prepared an organizational change for Secretarial approval to alter the program levels structure of DCE and DCBD and revise the divisional functional statement of DCPC.

- Manual Issuances: Prepared the following policy issuances for the NCI Manual:
    - Procedures for ADP/OA Hardware Inventory
    - Dissemination of Scientific and Professional Information by NCI Employees
    - Audit Procedures for Overtime Administration
    - Implementation of NCI Policy on Incomplete/Cancelled Training

OFFICE OF CANCER COMMUNICATIONS
OFFICE OF THE DIRECTOR
NATIONAL CANCER INSTITUTE

Program Activities Report
October 1, 1983 - September 30, 1984

The National Cancer Act Amendments of 1974 require that the "Director of the National Cancer Institute (NCI) shall provide and contract for a program to disseminate and interpret on a current basis for practitioners and other health professionals, scientists and the general public, scientific and other information respecting cause, prevention, diagnosis and treatment of cancer."

NCI disseminates information in three categories:

1. Scientific information used and produced by investigators.

2. State-of-the-art information for use of health professionals and the public.

3. Administrative and program information used by NCI and other organizations within the National Cancer Program.

The Office of Cancer Communications is a major source of information for the public (including cancer patients and people at risk of developing cancer), and a substantial source for health professionals. It carries out traditional communications support activities for NCI. Within the National Cancer Program, it assumes the role of coordinator of cancer communications, and develops new initiatives to help meet responsibilities stemming from the Act, to provide the public and health professionals with useful information about cancer.

OCC's traditional activities include responding to press inquiries; preparing news releases, press summaries, announcements, and background statements for use by the press; and assisting in press room operations at major cancer-related scientific meetings. The OCC develops reports and publications, speeches and congressional testimony, reports required by law, special reports for the byline of NCI's Director, and a wide variety of publications and audiovisual materials for public and professional audiences.

The OCC develops exhibits aimed primarily at health professionals and scientists. They are used at scientific and professional meetings each year, and provide audiences with information on cancer and how to tap resources available through NCI and other organizations.

The office also responds to public inquiries: those requiring both customized and non-customized written responses, and controlled and congressional inquiries. The office distributes publications, and replies to inquiries by regular telephon and to a special toll-free number.

OCC maintains awareness of communications activities of all participants in the National Cancer Program, assuring that there is a minimum of unneeded duplicatio and identifying and filling gaps in communications programming.

The OCC operates a national Cancer Information Clearinghouse that maintains awareness of cancer-related information and educational materials and services produced or used by the cancer community. The Clearinghouse responds to requests for information about available informational and educational materials and services, promotes the use of existing informational and educational materials and services, and identifies areas where needed materials and services do not exist.

OCC's approach to information dissemination is to reach out to target audiences through intermediary groups which have best access to the chosen audiences. The types of intermediary organizations with which OCC is involved are: cancer related (cancer centers, cancer societies); non-cancer related (fraternal organizations, medical societies, community groups, etc.); and the mass media. Major organized dissemination projects are under way in the areas of cancer prevention awareness, breast cancer information, coping with cancer, and special (minority) audiences. Other areas of special emphasis are: (1) pretesting and evaluation of all communications projects; (2) support for 22 Cancer Information Service offices located around the country; and (3) an internship program for graduate students in journalism, communications, etc.

As part of the development of needed communications resources, OCC sponsors a six-month graduate internship in health communications. Outstanding graduate students are selected for varied communications appointments involving science writing, information sciences and health education, and program administration. Interns are assigned to work with professional staff and are given writing, editing and a variety of other technical tasks. Interns are encouraged to participate in a seminar series and to develop special projects during their term.

J. Paul Van Nevel is the director of OCC, and Gertrude Anthony serves as secretary.

INFORMATION PROJECTS BRANCH

The Information Projects Branch (IPB) is responsible for designing, implementing, and evaluating programs to disseminate cancer information. As such, it has undertaken a variety of projects to reach various target audiences with specific health messages.

Cancer Prevention Awareness Program

Today we know that nearly 80 percent of cancers are related to environmental causes, many associated with personal behavior such as cigarette smoking and eating habits. Many of these cancers can be prevented if people adopt healthful behaviors that help protect against cancer.

However, a survey conducted by the National Cancer Institute (NCI) in June 1983 revealed that the public's view of cancer is confused; people are pessimistic about cancer risks and the potential for personal control over those risks. Many believe--quite erroneously--that "everything causes cancer" and that "there is not much a person can do to prevent it."

In March 1984, NCI publicly introduced the Cancer Prevention Awareness Program. Following a public announcement by DHHS Secretary Margaret Heckler, at a March 6 press conference, 2 1/2 million NCI prevention booklets were printed and background materials and public service messages were distributed nationwide to broadcasters, newspapers and magazines. In the first four months of the program, hundreds of media outlets carried cancer prevention messages (TV and radio public service announcements), as well as offered the prevention booklets via the toll-free 800 number of NCI's Cancer Information Service. In June, NBC network television produced a half-hour cancer prevention test show for 115 stations. The cover story of the July issue of the Saturday Evening Post was an interview with the NCI Director, focusing on diet and cancer prevention.

The Cancer Prevention Awareness Program is a major effort to increase public awareness of the possibilities for cancer prevention, presenting a challenge to the American people to learn what they can do every day to control their own cancer risks. Based on the most recent scientific information related to cancer and prevention, the program offers specific tips for individual action. Objectives of the program are:

- To improve public attitudes regarding cancer incidence, treatment, and prevention;
- To improve public awareness and knowledge of cancer risks and of individual actions that control some of those risks; and
- To encourage individuals to adopt healthy behaviors to reduce their cancer risks.

Messages: The program theme, "CANCER PREVENTION--The News Is Getting Better All The Time," encourages optimism. Messages emphasize personal control, explaining that individuals can take steps every day to control their own cancer risks. These steps are:

- Don't smoke or use tobacco in any form.
- If you drink alcoholic beverages, do so only in moderation.
- Eat foods low in fat.
- Include fresh fruits, vegetables, and whole grain cereals in your daily diet.
- Avoid unnecessary X-rays.
- Keep yourself safe on the job by using protective devices (respirators, protective clothing).
- Avoid too much sunlight; wear protective clothing; use sunscreens.
- Take estrogens only as long as necessary.

Scope of Program: The program is being implemented in two phases. Phase I relies primarily on mass media efforts to create awareness of prevention messages and to encourage people to learn about cancer prevention from a free NCI booklet available by calling 1-800-4-CANCER, the NCI Cancer Information Service. NCI is identified as a credible source of cancer risk information. Health professionals will be urged to discuss cancer prevention with their patients.

During May and June, seven regional meetings were held in conjunction with the Cancer Communication Network offices. The goal of these meetings was to bring in organizations, professional groups, voluntary agencies and other groups interested in cancer prevention, to introduce the Cancer Prevention Awareness Program and to elicit recommendations for developing education programs. Program emphasis will shift from the general public toward populations at greater than average risks (e.g., smokers). Organizations who serve these groups, especially at state and local levels, will be encouraged to conduct cancer prevention programs. Program messages and materials will explain risk factors and ways to reduce them.

Smoking Education Programs: The IPB is engaged in a number of projects intended to help smokers who want to quit, either directly or through health professionals; to assist school officials and others interested in education to develop smoking cessation programs for youth; to develop approaches to utilize the workplace and other settings for smoking cessation programs; to design education materials aimed at high-risk and minority audiences; and to stimulate smoking-related efforts through the print and audiovisual media. These activities are being developed and implemented in cooperation with other public and private health organizations, to assure that these smoking programs will contribute to an overall coordinated effort.

The following projects related to smoking are underway for health professionals:

1. "Quit for Good" kit. Intended for use by physicians and dentists with patients who want to quit smoking, this kit is an updated, combined, and streamlined version of two previous smoking cessation kits--"Helping Smokers Quit" (for physicians) and "Let's Help Smokers Quit" (for dental professionals). The new "Quit for Good" kit contains materials for counseling 50 patients and includes a brief booklet that contains general tips on counseling patients about not smoking and common questions and answers about smoking, a guide to help patients stop smoking, and a booklet to reinforce smoking behavior. Beginning in July 1984, the "Quit for Good" kit was announced through print ad and editorial coverage in medical and dental publications, direct mailing of a promotional flyer to more than 400,000 physicians and dentists, exhibits at professional meetings, and special promotions by participating professional organizations.

2. "Helping Smokers Quit" program. The American Pharmaceutical Association and the National Cancer Institute have worked together to design a smoking cessation program for pharmacists' use in counseling patients who would like to quit smoking. The program (similar to the quit-smoking kits designed for physicians and dentists) became available this year, with wide promotion beginning in September.

3. Smoking Programs for Youth. To fill a gap in the existing literature on smoking education for young people, OCC has prepared this comprehensive state-of-the-art report. This booklet discusses the issues related to adolescent smoking, and summarizes policies, curricula, and counseling programs related to smoking prevention/cessation in primary and secondary schools.

For public audiences, a booklet entitled Clearing the Air is available, which is a compilation of methods and techniques for quitting smoking. The booklet is also available in Spanish.

Breast Cancer Education Program

The goal of the Breast Cancer Education Program is to improve public knowledge, attitudes, and practices related to breast cancer in order to:

- Increase detection practices, including:
  - Instruction in breast self-examination (BSE) techniques by health professionals;
  - Thorough monthly breast self-examination;
  - Routine breast examination by a health professional; and
  - Mammography when recommended and appropriate.
- Reduce delay in seeking medical consultation for breast cancer symptoms.
- Improve the ability to deal effectively with the medical and psychosocial aspects of breast disease should a symptom be discovered.

The audience for the program is all women over age 18, with materials prepared and tested especially for women at increased risk to breast cancer and women who tend to have lower levels of knowledge about the subject. Individual programs are based on extensive evaluation of previous breast cancer education programs; results of NCI's national survey of public knowledge, attitudes, and practices related to breast cancer; and careful pretesting among target audiences.

Public education programs and materials:

"Breast Cancer: We're Making Progress Every Day." This public education program (formerly entitled "Progress Against Breast Cancer") is designed for use by businesses, service clubs, religious organizations, unions, and other interested groups. Program materials include:

A slide/tape or videocassette program providing an overview of the progress being made in breast cancer detection, diagnosis, treatment, and breast reconstruction; a pamphlet, "Breast Cancer: We're Making Progress Every Day," for each member of the audience which summarizes the information contained in the program and contains step-by-step instructions on how to perform BSE: two posters for display; a "User's Guide" to help those organizing the program; a print ad featuring movie critic Gene Shalit's review of the program; and the Breast Cancer Digest.

"Breast Exams: What You Should Know." Describes a variety of breast cancer screening methods including physical examination, mammography, and breast self-examination (BSE). Also available in Spanish.

"Questions and Answers About Breast Lumps." Discusses some of the most common noncancerous lumps, diagnostic procedures, treatment, and cancer risks.

"If You've Thought About Breast Cancer." Written by Rose Kushner, this booklet contains information about symptoms of breast cancer, detection diagnosis, treatment, rehabilitation, breast reconstruction, and other information helpful to breast cancer patients and their families.

"Breast Cancer: We're Making Progress Every Day." Summarizes current information about breast cancer, including risks and signs of the disease; mammography, biopsy, and treatment options; breast reconstruction; and rehabilitation. An illustrated guide for BSE is also included. This pamphlet is a revised version of "Progress Against Breast Cancer."

"What You Need to Know About Cancer of the Breast." This pamphlet discusses symptoms, diagnosis, rehabilitation, emotional issues, and questions to ask a doctor.

Patient education programs and materials:

A. Breast Cancer Patient Education Series. To help meet the information and education needs of breast cancer patients and their family members, NCI developed a sequential, 11-unit series of patient education materials. The series is designed to follow eight critical intervention points when information most often helps the patient: breast evaluation, biopsy, primary treatment, adjuvant therapy, followup care, breast reconstruction, recurrent disease, and advanced disease. The series consists of the following materials:

1. "Breast Exams: What You Should Know."

2. "Questions and Answers About Breast Lumps."

3. "Breast Biopsy: What You Should Know"--Discusses the one- and two-step procedures, what to expect in the hospital, awaiting the diagnosis, and coping with the possibility of breast cancer.

4. "Breast Cancer: Understanding Treatment Options"--Summarizes the biopsy procedure, types of breast surgery (giving advantages and disadvantages for each), radiation therapy as primary treatment, and making treatment decisions.

5. "Mastectomy: A Treatment for Breast Cancer"--Presents information about the different types of breast surgery, what to expect in the hospital, during the recovery period, and coping with having breast surgery. BSE for mastectomy patients is also described.

6. "Radiation Therapy: A Treatment for Early State Breast Cancer"--Discusses the treatment steps (lymph node surgery, radiation therapy, and booster radiation); possible side effects; precautions to take after treatment; and emotional adjustment to having breast cancer.

7. "Adjuvant Chemotherapy: A Breast Cancer Fact Sheet"--Describes the drugs, treatment plan, side effects, and outlook for breast cancer patients receiving this form of treatment.

8. "After Breast Cancer: A Guide to Followup Care"--For the woman who has completed treatment, this booklet explains the importance of continuing BSE, regular physical exams, possible signs of recurrence, and managing the physical and emotional side effects of having had breast cancer.

9. "Breast Reconstruction: A Matter of Choice"--Discusses the techniques used in breast reconstruction, possible complications, answers to common

questions, criteria for choosing a plastic surgeon, and issues of emotional adjustment.

10. "When Cancer Recurs: Meeting the Challenge Again"--Details the different types of recurrence, types of treatment, and coping with cancer's return.

11. "Advanced Cancer: Living Each Day"--Addresses living with a terminal illness, how to cope, and practical considerations for the patient, family, and friends.

B. Programs and materials for health professionals or program planners. "BSE-In-Hospital." This audiovisual program is designed to help nurses teach hospitalized women how to perform breast self-examination (BSE) and to encourage these women to practice BSE monthly following their hospital stay. Field-test results indicate that women who receive BSE instruction by a health professional report higher rates of BSE practice than those taught by any other method. In addition, these women felt more confident doing BSE and did a more thorough job of examining their breasts. The program has been endorsed by the American Society for Nursing Service Administrators. Program materials include:

"Coordinator's Guide" which provides suggestions on how to implement the program in the hospital setting; a three-part slide/tape or videocassette program covering the progress being made against breast cancer, information on the anatomy and physiology of the breast, and instructions on how to teach patients to do BSE; a brochure for nurses, "Teaching Breast Self-Examination," which reinforces the information in the program; a pamphlet for patients, "Breast Exams: What You Should Know," describing BSE using step-by-step illustrations; a series of four posters for nurses' stations and lounges to remind them to teach their patients BSE; a certificate for nurses that may be awarded upon completing the training program; and The Breast Cancer Digest.

The Breast Cancer Digest. This newly revised book is written for all members of the breast cancer health care team. It covers the current medical, psychosocial, and educational aspects of breast cancer including detection, diagnosis, treatment, rehabilitation, and breast reconstruction.

Breast Cancer: A Measure of Progress in Public Understanding. This publication is a management summary of NCI's national survey on public knowledge, attitudes, and practices related to breast cancer. The survey was conducted in 1979 among a national probability sample of women and men and a supplemental sample of urban black and Hispanic women. The survey has important implications for health program planners and health professionals.

Standards for Public Education on Breast Cancer. This publication is designed to provide direction for developing public information and education materials and programs about breast cancer. It synthesizes the most current data available on public knowledge, attitudes, and behavior related to breast cancer; addresses the implications of these data for public information program planning; and provides recommendations for program objectives, target audiences, and communications strategies.

Coping with Cancer Program

The goal of NCI's efforts in the Coping with Cancer Program is to provide those with cancer and their family members the opportunity to gain a sense of control over their lives by giving them information on the disease, its treatment, and psychosocial aspects. Program materials emphasize the following:

1. A diagnosis of cancer should not be considered a death sentence.

2. Living with cancer is frequently accompanied by physical, psychological, and/or social problems. Those with cancer and their families and friends can help themselves lead lives of quality by learning and adopting some useful coping strategies and behaviors.

3. Often, problems in coping with cancer and other chronic diseases are not unique, but are common to many people. However, the usefulness of a particular coping strategy depends on individuals and their circumstances.

The primary audience for the program and the main focus for its materials are those with cancer and their families. The secondary audience includes health professionals and others to whom the patient and family go for care, information and support.

The following materials are available for adults with cancer and their families:

1. Eating Hints--Recipes and Tips for Better Nutrition During Cancer Treatment is a collection of helpful, practical information on making mealtime more pleasant for the patient. Tips for coping with common eating problems and tasty recipes are included in this cookbook-style publication.

2. Chemotherapy and You--A Guide to Self-Help During Treatment addresses problems and concerns associated with chemotherapy treatment. Emphasis is on explanation and self-help. Includes a glossary of terms.

3. Radiation Therapy and You--A Guide to Self-Help During Treatment addresses problems and concerns of patients in radiation treatment. Emphasis is on explanation and self-help. Includes a glossary of terms.

4. Taking Time--Support for People with Cancer and the People Who Care About Them is a sensitively written booklet for persons with cancer and their families, addressing the feelings and concerns of others in similar situations and how they have learned to cope.

5. Control of Cancer Pain is a fact sheet addressing medical and nonmedical modalities of dealing with pain related to cancer.

6. Questions and Answers About Pain Control was developed in cooperation with the Yale Comprehensive Cancer Center. This booklet was printed by and is available from the American Cancer Society. Includes information on pharmacologic (with medication) and nonpharmacologic (without medication) options for pain relief.

7. What You Need to Know About Cancer is a series of pamphlets discussing symptoms, diagnosis, rehabilitation, emotional issues, and questions to

ask the doctors. This series consists of one general pamphlet and two site-specific pamphlets.

The following materials are available for young people with cancer and their families:

1. Young People with Cancer: A Handbook for Parents was written in cooperation with the National Candlelighters Foundation. Includes information on the most common pediatric cancers, treatments, and side effects. Special consideration is given to the emotional impact of cancer on patients and family members.

2. Help Yourself: Tips for Teenagers with Cancer was produced in cooperation with Adria Laboratories, Inc. Includes a booklet and an audiotape designed to provide information and support to adolescents with cancer. Issues addressed include reactions to diagnosis, relationships with family and friends, school attendance, and body image. A User's Guide for health professionals is also available.

3. Hospital Days, Treatment Ways was developed for children with cancer. This coloring book explains procedures the young patient may experience in the hospital environment.

4. Diet and Nutrition: A Resource for Parents of Children with Cancer contains suggestions for dealing with nutrition problems arising from pediatric cancer or its treatment. Includes special diets and an attractive poster for convenient display in the kitchen.

5. What You Need to Know About Wilms Tumor; Child Leukemia--see Item 7 in section above.

The following materials are available for health professionals and others who provide support and information:

1. Coping with Cancer--A Resource for the Health Professional is a reference work on the psychological and social aspects of cancer. Summarizes issues faced by cancer patients of all ages and their families, and provides practical guidance to caregivers in responding to patient and family needs. Support programs available throughout the country are described. References for further reading and an easy-to-use subject index are included.

2. Students with Cancer--A Resource for the Educator is a booklet for educators of young students with cancer designed to answer questions pertaining to the student's participation in school activities.

3. Services Available to Persons with Cancer--National and Regional Organizations is a reprint from the October 10, 1980, Journal of the American Medical Association, written to acquaint the physician with national and regional organizations with services available to help patients with the psychological, social and economic problems related to their having cancer.

4. Help Yourself: Tips for Teenagers with Cancer: User's Guide is a short leaflet, produced in cooperation with Adria Laboratories, Inc., summariz-

ing the content included in the "Help Yourself" patient booklet and audiotape. The guide describes how patient materials can be used and provides discussion topics related to the audiotape.

5. Adult Patient Education in Cancer is a reference work on the state-of-the-art of adult cancer patient education. Points out those issues that create the special needs of cancer patients. Programs and activities for meeting these needs, as well as planning and evaluation, are discussed.

Pretesting and Evaluation Program

The pretesting and evaluation efforts center on assessing print and broadcast health messages, to insure that they are understandable to the public.

1. Two handbooks have been distributed widely, describing methods for evaluating health messages:

   Making PSA's Work. A handbook on developing and pretesting effective broadcast public service projects, based on results of the 4-year health message testing service project.

   Pretesting in Health Communications. Describes a model for developing health messages and outlines the major methods for pretesting print and broadcast messages.

   In addition, a handbook for conducting a broadcast pretest with an accompanying tape is being prepared.

2. A number of requests for technical expertise and support were made by a variety of health-concerned agencies during the year. All were supported with advice, consultation, and appropriate materils, including relevant publications and test reports.

The staff of the Information Projects Branch consists of Rose Mary Romano, branch chief; Barbara D. Blumberg, Eva Sereghy, Bill Morrison and Joan Houghton, program staff; and Dorothy Kipnis and Rose Soodak, support staff. In May 1984, Nancy Nam, summer student, returned for a fifth summer. Five interns trained in the branch, as part of the OCC internship program: Blake Brown and Thomas Henderson (July-December 1983); Anne Mulbry and Joy Wilson (January-June 1984); and Anna-Lisa Robbert (July-December 1984).

REPORTS AND INQUIRIES BRANCH

The Reports and Inquiries Branch responds to inquiries from the public, cancer patients, and the news media, and disseminates information on research findings and National Cancer Institute activities. Information dissemination occurs in a variety of forms, including reports and other publications, speeches and congressional testimony, magazine articles, and news releases and fact sheets for the news media.

Robert M. Hadsell, Ph.D., is branch chief, with Mary Federline serving as secretary.

Reports Section

As in recent years, inquiries from the news media continued at a high level, reflecting interest in all areas of cancer research and activities of the National Cancer Institute and the National Cancer Program (NCP). Section staff responded to more than 3,000 inquiries from journalists, representing daily and weekly newspapers, magazines, and the electronic media, as well as newspapers and magazines for physicians and scientists. In addition, section staff initiated contacts with the media on numerous occasions to remind them of upcoming meetings, press conferences, or major reports. NCI administrators and scientists were interviewed for news and comment programs of the major television and radio networks, as well as local stations throughout the country and news organizations from many countries of the world. The documented telephone workload in the section showed an average call load of 11 to 15 calls per day to the person taking press calls, and an average of 640 calls per month coming into the section. From October 1983 through June 1984, the heaviest months for press calls were March and April; the lightest months were October and December. The most frequent calls were for interviews with NCI scientists, general information about cancer, cancer statistics, diet, nutrition and cancer, cancer prevention, reproductive cancers (especially breast cancer), and the Human T-Cell Leukemia/Lymphoma Virus (HTLV). Press inquiries continued at a high level as well on potential and known risks for cancer, Kaposi's sarcoma, AIDS, experimental cancer therapies, chemoprevention, and NCI priorities and budget.

Section staff assisted the American Society of Clinical Oncology (ASCO) in the press room operations at its annual meeting. Six summaries of NCI research findings were prepared, on systemic therapy for locally advanced breast cancer, the prospective diagnosis of malignant melanoma in a population at high risk; trials on adjuvant chemoterhapy and limb-sparing surgery in patients with high-grade soft-tissue sarcomas of the extremities; a trial of high-dose cisplatin, vinblastine, bleomycin, and VP-16 for poor prognosis nonseminomatous testicular cancer; secondary leukemia after treatment of childhood cancers with alkylating agents; and use of recombinant leukocyte A interferon in the treatment of advanced refractory cutaneous T-cell lymphomas. For the annual meeting of the American Association of Cancer Research (AACR), section staff prepared a summary of the Richard and Hinda Rosenthal Foundation Award lecture by John Minna on laboratory work of potential clinical importance in lung cancer; and a summary on research on malignant melanoma in Hodgkin's disease patients.

Reporters and researchers for television networks, film companies, and major newspapers continued major surveys of progress in cancer. NOVA and PBS prepared national documentaries on research on AIDS, focusing prominently on the work of NCI's Dr. Robert Gallo. There were increased numbers of inquiries this year on monoclonal antibodies, oncogenes, a NCI study of beer drinking as a risk factor in rectal cancer, and on cancer risks associated with tobacco, EDB (ethylene dibromide), and nuclear testing.

To respond more effectively to high levels of requests about evolving NCI research studies, section staff prepared 8 updates, 6 backgrounders, and 16 fact sheets, 12 of which were prepared as chapters for an upcoming book, Cancer Rates & Risks. One of the updates, "NCI Isolates AIDS Virus," and an accompanying detailed question and answer sheet, were prepared for the April 1984 announcement by DHHS Secretary Margaret Heckler of the virus's isolation.

Updates: NCI Isolates AIDS Virus, April 1984; Normal Human Oncogene Regulates Production of Human Growth Factor, March 1984; New Publication: Trends for Cancer Deaths by County, 1950-1979, February 1984; Human Tumor Viruses: the Search for Some is Over, January 1984; Study Links Lifestyle and Colon Cancer, January 1984; Leukemia Following Treatment with Methyl-CCNU for Gastrointestinal Cancers, November 1983; Cancer Patient Survival Statistics, November 1983; PDQ, Revised Summer 1984; and Ovarian Cancer, Summer 1984.

Cancer Rates and Risks: Drugs That Cause Cancer, March 1984; Breast Cancer, January 1984; Viruses and Cancer, December 1983; and Ionizing Radiation, December 1983; Non-Hodgkin's Lymphomas, December 1983; Cancer of the Uterine Cervix, December 1983; Cancer of the Uterine Corpus (Endometrium), December 1983; Cancers of the Urinary Tract, December 1983; Oral Cavity and Pharynx Cancers, December 1983; Pancreatic Cancer, December 1983; Testicular Cancer, November 1983; Ovarian Cancer, October 1983; Brain and Other Nervous System Cancers, October 1983.

Other Fact Sheets: The National Cancer Institute, Summer 1984; PET Imaging, Summer 1984; NMR, Summer 1984; Noninvasive Imaging, Summer 1984.

Backgrounders: National Cancer Institute Clinical Trials of Interferon, revised Summer 1984; Oncogenes, Summer 1984; Breast Cancer Screening, December 1983; Chemoprevention, revised Summer 1984; Biological Response Modifiers Program, revised Summer 1984; Tumor Invasion and Metastasis, Summer 1984.

In addition, section staff prepared NCI input for NIH special reports on NCI-sponsored research accomplishments in aging, diabetes, arthritis, sexual diseases, and AIDS; a revision of the NCI component of the NIH Almanac, and an introductory speech, Note to Reporters, and NIH Record story on the annual NIH Dyer lecture, given in November 1983 by Dr. Robert Gallo of NCI.

In addition to Cancer Rates and Risks, a continuing major effort of the past year was additional interviews, reviews and other research during preparation of a booklet for patients explaining clinical trials. This publication is now being published and should be available in late 1984. Other special activities were undertaken to educate women's groups concerning an NCI clinical trial of early breast cancer, such as stimulating interest in the study with the Women's Health Roundtable, the Christian Broadcast Network, and the Saturday Evening Post magazine.

Another special project was preparation of The Fast Food Fiber Guide as part of the NCI Cancer Prevention Awareness Program. The booklet is scheduled for publication in late 1984.

Section staff participated in the preparation of materials for Congress. Specific projects included the traditional statements for both the House and Senate appropriations hearings.

Staff also prepared the annual reports of the National Cancer Advisory Board (NCAB) and the President's Cancer Panel, and input for the NCI Director's annual report to the Congress.

In addition to several short articles for the NCI director, such as articles for U.S. Medicine and the Maryland Journal, staff prepared a speech for the director

The response to these efforts was consistently strong throughout the year and reflected the public's increasing knowledge about and interest in reliable information on cancer. In FY 1984 (the last two months projected), the section responded to 266,252 written and telephone inquiries, which included: 5,051 individually prepared custom letters; 255 "controlled" letters for members of Congress, the White House, and other government offices; 150,189 noncustom publication requests; 1,375 Cancer Information Clearinghouse requests; and 109,382 Cancer Information Service (CIS) telephone calls, up 69 percent from the 75,000 calls in 1983. In addition, more than 13 million publications were distributed in FY 1984, up 3 million from FY 1983.

The rise in telephone calls is the single most dramatic increase in the program over the previous year. The increase was due largely to public service announcements (PSA's) on television and radio giving the toll-free CIS number. These PSA's included announcements by the Surgeon General promoting antismoking materials and a publication entitled Cancer Facts for People Over 50. Other PSA's featured the new prevention booklet, Good News, and precautions to take in the summer sun. In addition, the CIS number was promoted in numerous weekly and monthly magazines, including Good Housekeeping, U.S. News and World Report, The National Enquirer, Redbook, Self, Glamour, Better Homes and Garden, and Women's Day.

Smoking remains a subject that generates many requests for publications, with more than 700,000 copies of Clearing the Air sent out in FY 1984. The new Cancer Prevention Awareness Program, which was launched in March, has generated about 856,000 requests for the prevention booklet, Good News. Approximately 630,000 copies of Breast Exams: What You Should Know were distributed during the year. About 22 million NCI publications representing 300 titles are stored at any one time in the 50,000-square-foot warehouse and distribution center. An inventory of these titles is maintained on the NIH Division of Computer Research and Technology (DCRT) computer system.

Because of the growing size and complexity of the public inquiries program, a number of quality control measures have been implemented. To assist the staff in finding accurate, up-to-date information to provide inquiries, the section's contractor developed a computerized index of sources of information. Topics are indexed from NCI publications, reference files, and from testimony and speeches given by the NCI Director. Updated printouts of the index have proved so helpful to the staff that the index is now sent regularly to all the regional CIS offices In addition, the contractor is also developing software programs for improved activity reports and enhanced inventory control.

Test calls are made to the CIS on a regular basis as part of program evaluation in the Cancer Communications Network. Reports on these calls are shared with the CIS staff as a means of continuing staff training.

During the year, the section initiated a special project to evaluate custom letters and bulk publication distribution. Questionnaires are sent with samples of written replies to letters from patients and the general public, and to a sample of the bulk publication mailings. Preliminary results indicate the public is well pleased with our service. They find the letter responses to be understandable, relevant, helpful and timely. Most bulk publication shipments have reached recipients within 11 days, with only two percent damaged on arrival.

for the Spring commencement of the George Washington University Medical School, and two lengthy letters to publishers of books explaining inaccuracies in the books' descriptions of cancer research and cancer treatment.

Section staff handled all publicity and coordinated preparation of materials and mailings to professionals and the media for two NIH Consensus Conferences: "Precursors to Malignant Melanoma", October 24-26, 1983; and "Limb-Sparing Treatment of Adult Soft Tissue and Osteogenic Sarcomas," to occur December 3-5, 1984.

More than 50 articles of interest to the NCI and NIH communities were prepared for the NIH Record, as well as two articles for the "From the NIH" column in the Journal of the American Medical Association.

The section issued quarterly a list of cancer-related meetings that is sent out to all NCI section chiefs, branch chiefs, and program directors.

Current permanent staff are Patricia Newman, section chief; writers Harriet Page, Alice Hamm, Linda Anderson, Eleanor Nealon, Florence Karlsberg, Joyce Doherty and Frank Mahaney; editorial assistants Amelia Champion and Anne Gooding; clerk-typist Marilyn Pazornik, and secretary Vivian Moses. Senior writer Lorraine Kershner continued her detail with the Public Health Service. Chris Hartman again worked in the section as a clerk-typist for the summer.

Five science-writing interns trained in the section, as part of the OCC internship program: Leslie Fink and Michele Gauthier (July - December 1983), Steve Benowitz and Conrad Storad (January -June 1984), and Steve Weiss (July - December 1984).

Public Inquiries Section

The Public Inquiries Section answers written and telephone inquiries about cancer from patients, their families, the general public, students, health and other professionals, and members of Congress and other government agencies. With the assistance of a contractor, Biospherics, Inc., the section prepares responses to written inquiries, operates the Cancer Information Service (CIS), a national toll-free telephone program that serves as backup to the Institute's Cancer Communications Network (CCN), and distributes publications in response to written and telephone requests.

The section's services are based on the National Cancer Act's philosophy that the American public should be provided the most accurate, up-to-date information about cancer cause, prevention, diagnosis, and treatment. The section provides information that combines standard, prepared materials with information tailored to the specific needs of each inquirer.

In general, the volume of letters, telephone inquiries, and publications distributed reflects the amount of media attention given to cancer, as well as OCC's promotion of cancer information through intermediaries. For instance, in 1984 the section began promoting and distributing information about cancer prevention, including smoking and other aspects of lifestyle that can cause cancer. Publicity campaigns and publications emphasize these subjects, all of which are designed to contribute to the Institute's national goal to reduce cancer mortality by 50 percent of today's rate by the end of the century.

Audio/Visuals Services. Videotapes were produced for use by the news media, to accompany reports on subjects such as: (1) HTLV Virus and its association with AIDS; (2) Oncogenes; (3) general background footage in the Laboratory of Pathology; and (4) NIH grounds and buildings. Photo support was furnished to major domestic and international print media to be used with cancer articles.

Special Communications. NCI's "Special Communication" is a service for rapid dissemination of information. The special communication is sent selectively to medical and voluntary groups, professional societies, and persons in allied health professions. During FY 1984, approximately 1 million individuals and groups were reached via special communications.

Publications Distribution Support. More than 1 million publications were distributed for NCI by Supermarket Communications Systems, Inc., in "Good Neighbor" bulletin boards located in 4,847 supermarkets and discount stores throughout the United States. The Consumer Information Distribution Center in Pueblo, Colorado, distributed 200,000 copies of NCI publications. More than 225 nonresearch materials, including publications, publication revisions, fact sheets and updates, special communications, NIH Record articles, press summaries, audiovisuals, and speeches, were processed by the section for official clearance.

Newsclipping Services. The section provided a daily newspaper clipping service of items of NCI interest to the professional staff, Cancer Information Service offices, and members of the President's Cancer Panel and the National Cancer Advisory Board. Section staff screened eight newspapers and a number of mass-circulation and scientific magazines and journals. Representative subjects given extensive coverage included AIDS research, cancer prevention through diet, increased control of environmental hazards including smoking, and organizations profiteering from cancer.

Freedom of Information Act Coordination. Under the Freedom of Information Act, 200 requests were received and processed. Approximately 600 Privacy Act requests were handled during the year. The FOI Coordinator responded to seven sets of interrogatories including microfilming volumes of grant applications. This effort proceeded with the cooperation of the U.S. Department of Justice.

Special Events. The NCI Awards Ceremony was held in October. Arrangements for the program and reception for the dedication of the R.A. Bloch International Cancer Information Center were handled by the section chief. Tours of NCI laboratories were arranged for international visitors.

Speakers Bureau. More than 100 participants from NCI and across the country are now members of NCI's Speakers Bureau. These doctors, oncologists, biomedical scientists, and cancer-related workers have volunteered their expertise and speaking abilities. The Speakers Bureau system is computerized by cancer topic. Also, a geographic file is available to provide speakers in local areas to various parts of the Nation. More than 50 speakers were provided to requestors such as cancer groups, colleges, civic organizations, and companies.

The staff of the section included Margaret Layton, section chief; Arlene Soodak-Cohen, visual information specialist; Alexia Roberts, NCI Freedom of Information coordinator; public affairs specialists Anthony Anastasi and Edith Gaub; and Beverly Gamble, secretary and purchasing clerk for the OCC. Ms. Kimberly Woodard served as a summer employee.

This year the section prepared a number of publications and fact sheets including: In Answer to Your Questions About Polycythemia Vera; Economic Impact of Cancer; Lasers in Cancer Treatment; Agent Orange; Fact Sheet--VP-16; Research Report on Leukemia; and Research Report on Prostate Cancer.

The section staff consisted of Robert M. Hadsell as acting chief until May, when Carol Case was appointed chief. She and Betty MacVicar, writer, are co-project officers of the Biospherics contract. The other permanent section staff are Joan Chamberlain, writer and director of the OCC Internship Program; and two secretaries, Liz Orellana and Sheila Stempler.

Five communication interns worked in the section during this fiscal year. Margie Rittman from Wayne State University and Lee Tune from the University of Alabama, July-December 1983; Sue Tripp from the University of California-Irvine and Bruce Hamren from Calilfornia State University at Chico, January-July 1984; and Janet Hansen from the University of Maryland, July-December 1984.

INFORMATION RESOURCES BRANCH

The Information Resources Branch is responsible for supporting OCC and NCI programs with a variety of information services. The branch has two sections. The Graphics and Audiovisuals Section manages printing, audio/visual services, and publication distribution, and oversees a variety of efforts such as FOI/Privacy Act coordination, NCI "Current Clips," Speakers Bureau, and the supermarket communications program. The Document Reference Section is a specialized information center serving the OCC. It responds to staff inquiries by using databases and maintaining a library of books, journals and other reference materials.

Joseph Bangiolo is branch chief, with Patricia Kelly serving as branch secretary since April 1984.

Graphics and Audiovisuals Section

The Graphics and Audiovisuals Section provides a variety of services to OCC and other NCI program areas.

Printing/Graphics Management Services. Printing management services are available for public information materials and other NCI publications produced throughout the Institute. This work involves coordination of graphics and printing services as well as arranging for distribution by direct mail.

NCI Exhibit Program. New table-top exhibits were developed on specific information programs. A new exhibit structure was prepared on "Advances in Cancer Research," for use in the OCC exhibit program. Exhibits were shown at 12 major professional meetings, and more than 100,000 publications were distributed. Printed materials were provided for health-related groups interested in cancer information. Other displays (bulletin boards) were produced for the three floors of building 31 where NCI personnel are located. Approximately six such displays were produced during the year. One exhibit was prepared featuring the PDQ information system, for display at the R. A. Bloch International Cancer Information Center.

Cancer Information Clearinghouse

The Information Resources Branch is responsible for the Cancer Information Clearinghouse. The clearinghouse is a source of information on cancer-related materials for use in public and patient education.

During FY 1984 significant changes in the project included: (1) the updating of files of materials and texts; (2) the weeding of "non-current" materials produced earlier than 1979; (3) promotion of the availability of the Clearinghouse database; and (4) evaluation of user satisfaction.

Document Reference Section

The DRS is a central informational resource for OCC and the Institute. Materials (published and unpublished) are collected, indexed, and are available to specific users. The in-house collection comprises public/press inquiry records, news clips, scientific publications, audiovisuals, and other significant documents. The automated, bibliographic database, composed of data records for DRS collection items, may be searched on-line.

The DRS database has grown by nearly 6,000 items to a total of 55,000. Weeding of 5,000 older items was accomplished. Additionally, indexing of more than 1,000 NCI archival materials was completed. A microcomputer was purchased to aid with documenting serial receipt, routing and claiming of unreceived materials.

In addition to the DRS database, section staff provide access to other major health-relevant databases. These include databases sponsored by the National Library of Medicine (MEDLINE, PDQ, CANCERLINE, CLINPROT, etc.).

Access to current news databases such as Newsearch and NEXIS allows the DRS to support the Institute with data useful in public information work. DRS searches aided health communicators, scientist-administrators, and public information specialists in responding to inquiries and developing information projects.

Patti Dickinson is section chief. Staff includes Judy Lim-Sharpe and Joyce Connor, librarians. Susan Murphy, a student at Catholic University, joined the staff in July 1983 as an information intern. Irene Heisig, a student at the University of Wisconsin, served as an information intern from January through June 1984. In July, Tim Morris from Wayne State University began an internship in the section. Ms. Barbara Odle joined the staff in January 1984 on the Unpaid Work Experience Program. Ms. Odle, who is a graduate of Galludet College, is taking coursework in Library and Information Science.

ANNUAL REPORT
OFFICE OF THE DIRECTOR FOR PROGRAM PLANNING AND ANALYSIS (ODPPA)
NATIONAL CANCER INSTITUTE
OCTOBER 1, 1983 - SEPTEMBER 30, 1984

OFFICE OF THE DIRECTOR

The ODPPA provides leadership, consultation and direct participation in: program analysis, planning and evaluation; the design, development and support of management information systems; the analysis of all legislation that could have an impact on the NCI and the conduct of appropriate liaison with the Congress; and providing design, development, coordination, and supporting services for office automation and information planning (OA/IP) activities throughout the Institute. (The OA/IP unit is currently being staffed.)

Organizationally it is located in the Office of the Director (OD), NCI, to enable it more effectively to provide its services to all operating units of the NCI and, at the discretion of the Director, to non-Federal organizations participating in the National Cancer Program (NCP). Operationally, it carries out its responsibilities in close collaboration with NCI operating units, counterpart offices at the NIH and DHHS, and other Federal agencies as required.

The Office consists of two branches: the Systems Planning Branch (SPB) and the Management Information Systems Branch (MISB). The Legislative/Congressional Unit is part of the immediate OD. The SPB is staffed with professionals with formal training and experience in general management, planning, operations research, systems analysis, and evaluation. The MISB is staffed with professionals with training and experience in the design, implementation, operation, and support of management and technical information systems. The legislative/congressional activities are performed by a senior analyst with extensive knowledge and experience in the Federal legislative process, and congressional committees and staff operations assisted by a legislative reference specialist.

Although primary and continuing assignments are made to each branch or unit based on expertise required, the Office often operates on a project matrix system whereby staff members are assigned to specific projects to provide the mix of scientific and managerial talents required by much of the work performed by the Office. Thus, rather than an accounting by organizational units, this annual report describes activities and accomplishments in terms of the major areas of performance: Planning and Evaluation, Management Information Systems, Legislative Analysis/Congressional Liaison, Office Automation and Information Planning.

Historically, the OPPA has worked closely with NCI operational units on an as-requested basis to carry out its responsibilities. A more continuous link between the OPPA and the operating units is brought about by the NCI Large Planning Group. This group consists of at least one professional, programmatic person from each NCI division and the senior members of the OPPA staff. Regularly scheduled monthly meetings have been held to plan work, exchange information and select planning areas for future targeting and participate in the preparation of the Institute's major planning and evaluation documents.

There were a couple of personnel actions during the reporting period: Terri Davis became secretary to the MISB and Starr Mihill became secretary to the Legislative Congressional Unit.

PLANNING AND EVALUATION

The Systems Planning Branch has the primary responsibility for carrying out activities in the areas of planning and evaluation. These include the development and application of systems analysis, planning, evaluation, and operations research techniques to cancer research and control activities; providing direct support for the National Cancer Program planning at the national and individual program levels; and participating in NIH and Department level planning.

Staff directs planning meetings; participates as members of planning teams organized to develop individual program plans; works directly with program and administrative personnel in the development of operational plans; maintains liaison with program personnel; provides periodic consultation and directs efforts, as requested by program leaders, to revise and update both program and operating plans; provides education and training in the use of systems techniques; and works closely with the financial management staff during the budget preparation cycle to correlate budget preparation with existing plans.

Specific planning activities engaged in during the past year are described in the paragraphs that follow:

A. Requests for planning assistance were heavy during this year as OPPA continued to support the Division of Cancer Prevention and Control (DCPC). Plans for high priority areas of Chemoprevention, Diet and Nutrition, and Smoking and Health were completed and presented to the DCPC Board of Scientific Counselors and the National Cancer Advisory Board. The Methods plans for the programs were also completed. An interim report on the Occupational Cancer Program Plan has been prepared. The Division of Cancer Treatment's linear array and decision network for the Drug Development Program has been updated; the preclinical portion is complete and ready for review by the Division.

   Planning efforts are in progress for Detection and Diagnosis, Cancer Centers, and Rehabilitation.

   The original strategy was to integrate all DCPC program plans into a DCPC master plan. However, with the delineation of the National Goals for the Year 2000, all other planning activities were subordinated to develop a strategy for achieving these national goals. This will be a major effort for both OPPA and DCPC.

   Each planning group consists of representatives from the NCI Divisions conducting research in that particular area, as well as senior members of the OPPA staff. During program planning, considerable emphasis is placed on developing or refining evaluation criteria so that planning may be thoroughly integrated with evaluation.

B. Preparation of the National Cancer Program 1983 Director's Report/Annual Plan (DR/AP) for FY 1985-88 for submission to the President and Congress as required by law is in process. This report describes National Cancer Program progress during 1983, current activities, and planned efforts for the five-year planning period, including budget projections.

The 1983 Director's Report/Annual Plan is being markedly modified to include more planning information, particularly directed toward describing ways in which the Institute plans to achieve the national goals for the Year 2000. Planned activities will be laid out at the higher fiscal levels specified in the by-pass budget.

The 1983 Report will also include an expanded section on coordination of the National Cancer Program with additional information on the cancer-related activities of nonprofit, State, and industrial groups. The contribution of professional organizations to the National Cancer Program and data about other Federal agencies and the groups previously noted resulted in a more complete description of non-NCI activities.

After extensive internal and external review (NCAB, NIH, OMB, OASH, etc.) and incorporation of review comments, the report will be submitted to the Secretary for transmittal to the President and the Congress and will be distributed to research and educational institutions, voluntary organizations, and Federal, State, and local agencies involved in cancer-related activities.

Since the Director's Report/Annual Plan highlights accomplishments during the past year as well as forecasting future activities, it is a valuable reference tool for information on all aspects of the National Cancer Program.

C. Coordinated the preparation for NCI participation in the Director's (NIH) Forward Planning Review Session including: 1) development of agenda items; 2) preparation of a briefing book for the Director, NCI, and staff; and 3) coordinating and reporting action items which resulted from the Review Session discussions. The focus of the Review Session is to prepare the Director, NIH, for the upcoming congressional appropriation hearings and items to be discussed at that time. Agenda items for this year's sessions were divided into two categories: 1) high priority areas of scientific opportunity, and 2) other program issues likely to be raised at the appropriation hearings. Regarding high priority areas of scientific opportunity, 12 specific items were discussed including oncogenes, biochemical monoclonal antibodies, drug resistance, HTLV, National Goals for the year 2000, smoking, SEER, nutrition, prevention studies, biochemical approaches to cancer invasion and metastases, and chemoprevention. The rationale for according these areas high priority and their FY 1984, 1985, and 1986 funding were described.

As a followup to the Director's Review Session, OPPA staff coordinated the preparation of the NCI chapter of the 1986 NIH Research Plan. This plan consisted of an update of the high priority areas of scientific opportunity which were presented at the Director's Forward Planning Review session and a description of major program changes for FY 1986 (new initiatives, reductions, expansions of ongoing activities, and changes in emphasis).

D. Prepared the NCI Evaluation Plan which included a description of recently completed, ongoing, and planned Institute evaluative efforts (set-aside and nonset-aside). Assistance was provided to NCI staff in the development, implementation, and administration of 1% set-aside evaluation projects, including the preparation of close-out documents for completed projects.

Close-out submissions include an executive summary, assessment of benefits, and an impact statement describing the importance and implications of the study for the program and any decisions that have been or will be made as a result of the study. Progress reports are prepared for multiphase or long duration projects.

The proposed set-aside evaluation budget for FY 1984 was $1,947,000 involving 10 projects. Four new projects were proposed; the others were continuations or deferrals from previous years. All of the new projects, with a total FY 1984 budget of $525,000, have received approval from the Assistant Secretary for Planning and Evaluation.

Material was prepared for NCI participation in Evaluation Plan review sessions at OD, NIH and departmental levels. The Office also has responsibility for coordinating and reporting any NCI activity action items which result from Review Session discussions. Branch personnel attend and participate in all reviews.

Starting in FY 1985, no set-aside funds will be provided the BIDs. A funding policy is being established for NCI.

E. Coordinated the preparation of NCI's contribution to the FY 1983 Maternal and Child Health Inventory. The submission included a listing of NCI projects (grants, contracts, interagency agreements, and intramural projects) where there was a major emphasis on maternal and child health, a summary narrative describing NCI efforts in this area, and a table showing distribution of the numbers of projects and dollar amounts by mechanism of support. Total FY 1983 funding of $32,067,334 (174 projects) was reported.

F. Other staff activities included:

- Membership on the Steering Committee for Office Automation/Information Planning.

- Consultative services to divisions and OD, NCI in planning, information, and evaluation, and especially on the monitoring of support service contracts.

- Membership on the DHHS Nutrition Research Committee.

- Evaluation of the Frederick Cancer Research Facility data processing contractor which supports four other contractors as well as NIH and NCI staff.

- Project Officer on Support Services Contract which serves the OD, NCI. Considerable staff time is required for monitoring present contract plus the planned recompetition.

- Assistant Project Officer on a contract to determine how significant events in cancer research have been supported.

MANAGEMENT INFORMATION SYSTEMS

The Management Information Systems Branch (MISB) is responsible for

A. The design, implementation, maintenance and coordination of a network of Management Information Systems (MIS) which provide information on budget, personnel, space, travel, and other primarily administrative activities;

B. Coordination of a variety of NCI automatic data processing (ADP) activities; and

C. Consultation with Institute staff on the application of ADP technology to the administration and management of NCI resources.

The MIS is composed of a network of user oriented and managed systems which supports both individual operating areas and provides consolidated reporting of information across organizational lines. Systems are developed at the request of and with the participation of the user organizations. Current MIS systems support areas within the OD and several of the divisions with priority given to applications for the Office of Administrative Management.

Maintaining the operational status of current systems is the primary responsibility of MISB staff. System enhancements and development of new capabilities are provided as resources permit.

Typical components of MIS activities include development of specifications for changes to existing systems or for new applications; implementing programs or testing contractor-developed software; providing documentation which includes manuals for operators and maintenance programmers as well as system overviews; installing the software; training users; and resolving operational problems. Specific activities in this area during the year included:

A. Design and implementation of a Personnel Vacancy Applicant System for the Personnel Management Branch. This system collects vacancy, applicant, and merit promotion data; generates letters which acknowledge receipt of the applications and request any additional required information; generates the select/non-select and vancancy cancellation letters; prepares status and activity reports; and archives the data.

B. Modifications to the Personal Services Forecasting System to refine the special pay projections for Commissioned Officers, reduce timing problems, add a consolidated report, provide straight line projections of expenditures, and implement other adjustments to improve the accuracy of the forecasts. The Employment Plan module of the system was also modified to report FCRF data separately and restructure the reporting of the Visting Program and summer employees.

C. Extensive changes to the Operating Budget/Status System to prepare new summaries by budget activity, mechanism, and division by mechanism; incorporate data from prior years into the system; add a new budget level for the Small Business Allotment; add a capability to provide footnotes in the budget reports; add a third budget format to provide thrust detail within each division; provide automatic generation of the CAN list from the central CAN file and an associated header file; and implement other changes to improve operations.

D. Changes to the Gift Fund System to correct several operational problems.

E. Expansion of the DCT/DTP Contract Tracking System to include the Animal Program.

F. Modification of the NCI Employee Training System to provide additional reports to the Personnel Management Branch and the administrative areas, and expansion of the file to provide data for automatic submission to the NIH Training Office.

G. Expanding the FTE system installed in DCT program areas to allow area planned accessions and separations to be automatically consolidated into a single division report.

H. Modification of all versions of the Financial Data Reporting System (FDRS) to accomodate typical fiscal year changes. Enhancements included adding end-of-year projections to the DCBD system based on data from the FDRS file and input from the users; installing command procedures to simplify and reduce errors in the operations of the FDRS in OD; and combining DCE FDRS files with CIP input to produce CIP's Financial Plans which include actual and projected obligations for CIP in-house programs, extramural contracts and consultant services.

I. Redesign and implementation of the six separately-maintained systems composing the DCT FDRS to provide for easier maintenance and operation. In addition a command procedure was installed to allow operation by non-technical staff.

J. Addition of programs to the NCI Personnel System which summarize, for FMB, NCI employees by professional/technical/support, division, and ceiling status and which notify OCC of specified categories of actions. The Onboard Report was rewritten and a series of other modifications to the processing of actions was completed to meet the data requirements of the Personal Services Forecasting Systems, to handle actions not previously defined, and to more accurately reflect the actions processing of the Institute.

Coordination and consultation activities continued to increase in both the number of requests and the resources required to complete them. While many of these were completed informally and in a short period of time, the following reflect larger staff efforts:

A. Participating in the Office Automation/Information Planning (OA/IP) Steering Committee, serving as the alternate for the Chairman of the committee, assisting in staffing and establishing the office, and providing leadership and support for assigned OA/IP activities.

B. Chairing and providing technical support for the OA/IP Inventory Coordination Working Group which is developing requirements and procedures to collect information on hardware and software used in the Institute. Preparation of the finalized procedures for an NCI ADP/OA Hardware Inventory were postponed in order to incorporate new PHS requirements for reporting on ADP hardware. Coordinated the development of procedures for a complete physical inventory of all ADP and OA equipment within the Institute; and provided data entry and editing, initialization of the NCI inventory and generation of PHS required data from the NCI file.

C. As a member of the OA/IP Electronic Mail Working Group, participating in the design of the questionnaire used for data collection, in the selection of the population to be surveyed, in the analysis of the data and in the preparation of the final report.

D. As the NCI ADP Systems Security Coordinator, identifying of all NCI employees who satisfied the criteria for classification as either ADP-I or ADP-II as defined by Part 6 of the HHS ADP Systems Manual and providing position-related information to NIH.

E. Coordinating updates to NCI's FY 1985 Information Technology Systems Budget to provide more detailed information on ADP procurements.

F. Coordinating the NCI submission and the OD component of the FY 1986 Information Technology Systems Budget. This budget includes a five-year plan and modification of the prior year submission.

G. Coordinating the NCI submission to the new PHS ADP Planning and Inventory Data Base for systems and contracts. The purpose of this inventory is to provide information to PHS to access the need for proposed ADP systems, systems modifications, ADP contracts and ADP and word processing equipment.

H. Participating in the technical review of contract proposals and evaluation of hardware and software for several non-MIS applications within the OD.

I. Initiating and maintaining a directory of NCI WYLBUR MAIL users to encourage the use of electronic mail within the Institute.

Departmental approval to proceed with MIS development in NCI was given under the condition that project results could be transferred to other institutes at NIH and to other agencies. This effort was continued by converting NCI's FDRS for use by the NIMH. The system was installed for NIMH, the user trained, documentation prepared, and consultation continues to be provided to the user upon request. Consultation was also provided to NIADDK and NHLBI on systems previously transferred to them. Discussions were held with representatives from ASPER, NEI, NHLBI, DRR and FIC to explain NCI software, procedures, etc.

MISB staff receives programming support via contract. Major activities of the contract are reported in the accompanying narrative.

LEGISLATIVE ANALYSIS AND CONGRESSIONAL LIAISON

The categories of activities in this area of responsibility are described below followed by a brief summary of typical actions carried out by the NCI during the past year.

A. Monitored and analyzed all legislation with potential impact or significance for the NCI. During the past year, bills on a wide variety of subjects were tracked and analyzed, i.e., reauthorization bills, radiation compensation, heroin for cancer patients, risk assessment, and smoking and health effects.

B. Assisted in the preparation of congressional hearings where NCI staff were requested to testify. Prepared briefing materials for the Director, Deputy Director and others, reviewed testimony, attended hearings and prepared responses to follow-up questions. During the past year the Director of NCI testified regarding reauthorization bills and appropriations for FY 1985. The NCI Deputy Director testified before the House Energy and Commerce Subcommittee on Health and the Environment on the "Compassionate Pain Relief Act." The NCI Associate Director testified before the House Committee on Science and Technology Subcommittee on investigations and Oversight on Oncoge Research and Development.

C. Responded to numerous telephone, written and personal inquiries made by members of Congress and their staffs about NCI programs. Coordinated, when appropriate, such responses with the Department of Health and Human Services and the NIH.

D. Through written and verbal communication, kept the senior NCI staff briefed on current congressional and legislative activities. Also kept the National Cancer Advisory Board informed of relevant congressional and legislative matters. Responded throughout the year to inquiries from the NCAB about pending bills, particularly as such bills could affect the operation of the NCAB.

E. Arranged for meetings between NCI senior staff and members of Congress and their staffs.

F. The NCI legislative office now uses Legi-Slate, a computerized system for assisting in tracking legislation.

CONTRACT NARRATIVE
OFFICE OF THE DIRECTOR FOR PROGRAM
PLANNING AND ANALYSIS, NCI
FY 1984

CONTRACTOR: JRB Associates (Contract NIH-N01-CO-75390)

TITLE: Planning and Support Services for the National Cancer Program

CONTRACTOR'S PROJECT DIRECTOR: Ms. Carol L. Anglin

PROJECT OFFICER: Ms. Barbara R. Murray

OBJECTIVE: Provide the support services necessary to assist the Office of the Director, NCI, in meeting the expanded responsibilities established by the National Cancer Act of 1971 and subsequent amendments.

MAJOR ACCOMPLISHMENTS: The activities included support services for program planning, the preparation of briefing and presentation materials, administrative and logistical support to the Office of the Director for planning conferences and meetings, and assistance in the preparation of draft documents required to develop the National Cancer Institute's Directors Report/Annual Plan.

SIGNIFICANCE TO THE NATIONAL CANCER PROGRAM: The expanded scope and responsibilities of the National Cancer Program have imposed additional requirements for reporting, planning and analyzing alternative courses of action. This contract provides assistance in areas which could not be performed within NCI.

DATE CONTRACT INITIATED: September 30, 1977

TOTAL CONTRACT VALUE: $3,403,104 all of which has been obligated. The contract was scheduled to end July 1984. A terminal extension has been requested to allow sufficient time for a recompetition which is in process.

CONTRACT NARRATIVE
OFFICE OF THE DIRECTOR FOR PROGRAM
PLANNING AND ANALYSIS, NCI
FY 1984

CONTRACTOR: System Sciences, Inc. (N01-CO-33854)

TITLE: NCI Management Information Systems Support Services (Programming)

CONTRACTOR'S PROJECT DIRECTOR: Christopher Gordon

PROJECT OFFICER: Betty Ann Sullivan

OBJECTIVE: To provide technical support services to the Management Information Systems Branch in the expansion, maintenance, and operation of NCI's Management Information Systems and to support other computer-related activities of the Branch. Specific activities include preparation of detailed flowcharts, programming of computer routines, debugging and testing of programs, providing technical documentation, supporting operations and training users.

MAJOR ACCOMPLISHMENTS: The following activities were initiated during the year: implementation of a Personnel Vacancy Applicant System to assist PMB in the processing of recruitment actions; modifications to the Personal Services Forecasting System to improve the accuracy the forecasts and provide new reporting capabilities; extensive changes to the Operating Budget/Status System to provide new summaries, incorporate data from prior years, add a new budget level and a new format, and automatically generate the CAN list; expanding the NCI Employee Training System to provide new reports and automatic data submission to NIH; enhancing most versions of the FDRS; modifying the processing of actions in the NCI Personnel System; and providing extensive support for the initiation of the NCI ADP/OA Hardware Inventory. Support in implementing typical fiscal year changes and resolution of operational problems continued.

SIGNIFICANCE TO THE NATIONAL CANCER PROGRAM: The National Cancer Act of 1971 provided for improved information systems. This contract gives NCI the programming support required to maintain the operational status of the Management Information Systems, to implement new modules and to assist in coordination activities of the MISB.

PROPOSED COURSE: To continue the current pattern of maintenance, operational and development support for MISB activities.

DATE CONTRACT INITIATED: May 26, 1983

TOTAL VALUE OF CONTRACT: $673,898